ATLAS

3

Learning-Centered
Communication

David Nunan

Heinle & Heinle Publishers
A Division of International Thomson Publishing, Inc.
Boston, MA 02116, U.S.A.

I(T)P   The ITP logo is a trademark under license.

The publication of ATLAS was directed by the members of the Heinle & Heinle Global Innovations Publishing Team:

Elizabeth Holthaus, ESL Team Leader
David C. Lee, Editorial Director
John F. McHugh, Market Development Director
Lisa McLaughlin, Production Editor
Nancy Mann, Developmental Editor

Also participating in the publication of the program were:

Publisher: Stanley J. Galek
Assistant Editor: Kenneth Mattsson
Manufacturing Coordinator: Mary Beth Hennebury
Full-Service Design and Production: Ligature, Inc.

Manufactured in the United States of America.

ISBN: 0-8384-4087-8

Heinle & Heinle Publishers is a division of International Thomson Publishing, Inc.

10 9 8 7 6 5 4 3 2

Preface

Atlas is a four-level ESL/EFL course for young adults and adults. Its learner-centered, task-based approach motivates learners and helps to create an active, communicative classroom.

Atlas develops the four language skills of listening, speaking, reading, and writing in a systematic and integrated fashion. Each level is designed to cover from 60 to 90 hours of classroom instruction. It can also be adapted for shorter or longer courses; suggestions for doing so are provided in the teacher's extended edition.

Each level of Atlas consists of the following components:

Student's Book: The student's book contains 12 "core" units and 3 review units. Following the 15 units are "Communication Challenges," which provide extra communicative practice to conclude each unit. Grammar summaries for each unit appear at the end of the book, along with an irregular verb chart.

Teacher's Extended Edition. The teacher's extended edition contains an introduction to the philosophy of the course, general guidelines for teaching with Atlas, detailed teaching suggestions for each unit, and extension activities. It also includes the tapescript and answer keys for the textbook and the workbook.

Teacher Tape: The tape contains spoken material for all of the listening activities in the student text.

Workbook: The workbook provides practice and expansion of the vocabulary, structures, functions, and learning strategies in the student text.

Workbook Tape: The workbook tape contains spoken material for all of the listening activities in the workbook.

Video: The video, which contains lively, real-life material, provides reinforcement and expansion of the topics and functions found in the student text.

Assessment Package: The assessment package will be available in 1995.

FEATURES	BENEFITS
Unit goals are explicitly stated at the beginning of each unit.	Awareness of goals helps students to focus their learning.
Listening and reading texts are derived from **high-interest, authentic source material.**	Naturalistic/realistic language prepares students for the language they will encounter outside the classroom.
Each unit is built around two **task chains**, sequences of tasks that are linked together in principled ways and in which succeeding tasks are built on those that come before.	Task chains enhance student interest and motivation by providing students with integrated learning experiences.
Units feature explicit focus on **learning strategies**.	Conscious development of a range of learning strategies helps students become more effective learners both in and out of class.
End-of-unit **Self-Check** section encourages students to record and reflect on what they have learned.	Developing personal records of achievement increases student confidence and motivation.

Table of Contents

*The asterisked learning strategies are explicitly taught in the unit. The others are used passively.

ou're invited . . . go to the movies meet me for lunch
what do you do
why
is my family neighborhood

Language Focus Structures	Learning Strategies	Communication Challenges
• infinitives • superlative adjectives	• self-evaluation* • predicting • summarizing • selective listening • skimming	• Information gap: Interviews
• two-part verbs • indirect questions	• lateral thinking* • brainstorming • selective listening • making inferences • choosing • cooperating	• Information gap: Choosing a TV
• comparison of adverbs and adjectives • future: present progressive, *going to*	• top-down reading* • personalizing • selective listening • practicing • summarizing • scanning	• Guessing game: Travel plans
• *would rather, prefer* • passive voice	• grouping* • personalizing • selective listening • brainstorming • predicting • choosing	• Information gap: Unsatisfactory purchase
• prepositional phrases with *by* • word order of modifiers	• reflecting* • selective listening • cooperating • comparing • classifying • matching	• Interview: What's your learning style?

*The asterisked learning strategies are explicitly taught in the unit. The others are used passively.

Acknowledgments

Many people were involved in the planning and development of Atlas, and it is impossible for me to mention them all by name. However, special thanks must go to the following:

The reviewers, who helped to shape Atlas:

Lucia de Aragão, Uniao Cultural, São Paulo, **Eric Beatty**, Institut Franco-Américain, Rennes, **Rosamunde Blanck**, City University of New York, Hiroshima, **Richard Berwick**, University of British Columbia, Vancouver, **Jennifer Bixby**, Acton, Massachusetts, **Eric Bray**, YMCA English School, Kyoto, **Vincent Broderick**, Soai College, Osaka, **Chiou-Lan Chern**, Tunghai University, Taichung, **Katy Cox**, Casa Thomas Jefferson, Brasilia, **Richard Evanoff**, Aoyama Gakuin University, Tokyo, **Charles Frederickson, Katherine Harrington**, Associacao Alumni, São Paulo, **Phyllis Herrin de Obregon**, Universidade Autonoma de Querétaro, Querétaro, **James Kahny**, Language Institute of Japan, Tokyo, **Thomas Kanemoto**, Kanda Institute of Foreign Languages, Tokyo, **Maidy Kiji**, Konan Women's University, Kobe, **Richard Klecan**, Miyagi Gakuin, Sendai, **Susan Kobashigawa, Thomas Kral**, United States Information Agency, Washington, D.C., **David Levy**, McGill University, Montreal, **Angela Llanas**, Instituto Anglo-Mexicano, Mexico City, **Thomas Long**, ELS International, Seoul, **David Ludwig**, Crane Publishing Company, Taipei, **Carole McCarthy**, CEGEP ST-Hyacinthe, Quebec, **Jane McElroy**, University of Rio Grande, Tokyo, **John Moore and Aviva Smith**, ECC Foreign Language Institute, Tokyo, **Rebecca Oxford**, University of Alabama, Tuscaloosa, **Margene Petersen**, ELS, Philadelphia, Pennsylvania, **James Riordan and Adelaide Oliveira**, Associacao Cultural, Salvador, **Andrea Safire**, Berkeley, California, **Charles Sandy**, Chubu University Junior College, Nagoya, **Tamara Swenson**, Osaka Jogakuin Junior College, Osaka

The teachers and students in the following institutions, who field-tested early versions of Atlas and provided invaluable comments and suggestions:

AEON, Japan, **Aoyama Gakuin University**, Tokyo, **Associacao Alumni**, São Paulo, **Associacao Cultural**, Salvador, **Associacao Cultural**, Ribeirão Prêto, **AEON**, **Boston University**, Boston, Massachusetts, **Centro Cultural Brasil–Estados Unidos**, Campinas, **Concordia University**, Montreal, **ELS International**, Seoul, **GEOS**, Japan, **Huron University**, Tokyo, **Instituto Anglo-Mexicano**, Mexico City, **Konan Women's University**, Kobe, **LaGuardia Community College**, Long Island City, New York, **Miyagi Gakuin**, Sendai, **Osaka Jogakuin Junior College**, Osaka, **SHOWA Women's University**, Boston, Massachusetts, **Soai College**, Osaka, **Southwest Community College**, Los Angeles, **Tokyo Foreign Language College**, Tokyo, **Universidade Autonoma de Querétaro**, Querétaro, **Waseda University**, Tokyo, **YMCA English School**, Kyoto

Other reviewers, too numerous to mention, helped make this course what it is. Particular thanks must go to Ellen Shaw, who is quite simply the best editor in the business and whose detailed editing and comments strengthened the materials in many different ways. Thanks also to Clarice Lamb, whose unflinching faith in the project helped me maintain my own faith through periods of difficulty and doubt.

I should also like to acknowledge and thank the various International Thomson Publishing and Heinle & Heinle representatives who facilitated field testing and whose personal assistance during visits associated with the development and promotion of Atlas was invaluable. I should like to thank Robert Cullen in Singapore, Carol Chen in Taipei, and Hisae Inami in Tokyo for their particular assistance and support.

Particular thanks are due to my editors at Heinle & Heinle, who helped at all stages in the planning and development of Atlas. Special thanks are due to Charlie Heinle and Stan Galek, for their personal interest and support from the very beginning of the project; to José Wehnes, for his unique marketing philosophy; to Dave Lee, who helped guide the project; to Chris Foley, who helped shape the initial philosophy; to Meg Morris, for her research and data-gathering skills; and to Lisa McLaughlin, for her dedication to ensuring the visual appeal of the book. Most of all, thanks are due to my developmental editor, Nancy Mann, for her professional skills, her quiet good humor, and her happy acceptance of late-night calls.

1 The World of Work

Warm-Up

Picture 1

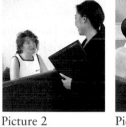
Picture 2

Picture 3

Picture 4

Picture 5

Picture 6

Picture 7

Unit Goals

In this unit you will:

Identify people

"The guy who spoke to you is the boss."

Discuss pros and cons of jobs

"Tania has an interesting job."

"I wouldn't like a boring job."

"I wouldn't mind an exciting job."

1 **Group Work** Discussion. Look at the pictures above. What are these people's jobs?

2 a Check [√] the words you know. Look up the others in your dictionary.

☐ tiring   ☐ amazing   ☐ boring   ☐ interesting
☐ exciting   ☐ depressing   ☐ fascinating ☐ surprising
☐ exhausting   ☐ satisfying   ☐ confusing

b **Group Work** The words above can describe jobs. Are the words positive, negative, or neutral? Make statements using these words and phrases: *wouldn't like, wouldn't mind,* or *would like.*

Positive	Negative
I would like . . .	I wouldn't like . . .
I wouldn't mind . . .	

3 **Group Work** Look again at the pictures above and make statements about each job.

Example: "Being an architect would be a satisfying job."

Task Chain 1
Have you met everyone?

Conversation ....

Conversation ....

Conversation ....

Task 1

a 🎧 Listen and write the number of each conversation under the correct picture.

b 🎧 Listen to Marcella. What is she talking about? Check [√] your response. Which words in the listening gave you the answer?

- ☐ her first date
- ☐ her first day at work
- ☐ her first day at school

Task 2

a Look at these words and phrases and check [√] the ones you don't know.

- ☐ take . . . coffee
- ☐ milk . . . sugar
- ☐ tell . . . people . . . office
- ☐ woman . . . sits . . . reception desk . . . know-it-all
- ☐ Scott . . . brings . . . paychecks
- ☐ Len . . . does . . . mail
- ☐ He's . . . office gossip
- ☐ woman . . . knows . . . good points . . . bad points

b You are going to hear these words in a conversation. Can you predict what the conversation is about?

c 🎧 Listen. Circle the words and phrases when you hear them.

Task 3

🎧 Listen again. What do you hear about these people? Fill in the chart.

PERSON	INFORMATION
Jane	*know-it-all*
Scott	
Len	
Marcella	

ou're invited ... go to the movies! meet me for lunch
what do you do?
why
when
s my family neighborhood

Task 4

a Pair Work Study the following statements and see if you can infer the meaning of the words in italics.

"The woman who sits at the reception desk is a real *know-it-all*. She has an answer for everything. This other guy is the office *gossip*. He talks about everyone."

b Group Work Compare your responses with another pair's responses.

Task 5

Group Work Here is a list of ten occupations. Try to order them from highest-paid to lowest-paid (1 to 10) in North America. Which jobs do you think are held mostly by men? Mostly by women? Check [√] the correct columns.

Occupation	*Men*	*Women*
.... teacher	☐	☐
.... airline pilot	☐	☐
.... chemical engineer	☐	☐
.... lawyer	☐	☐
.... pharmacist	☐	☐
.... social worker	☐	☐
.... architect	☐	☐
.... cashier	☐	☐
.... cab driver	☐	☐
.... plumber	☐	☐

Task 6

You choose: Do **A** or **B**.

A Look at the answers on page 115 and check your responses to Task 5. Do you think that the responses would be the same for your country? What would be similar? What would be different?

B Look at the answers on page 115 and check your responses to Task 5. What do you think of these occupations? Can you pick a word from the Warm-Up for each occupation?

Task 7

Make a list of the pros and cons of one of the jobs in Task 5 and talk about it.

"Well, I think that being an airline pilot would be exciting. The salary is good, and you get to travel around a lot. On the other hand, you'd be away from your family a lot, and sitting around in airports would be pretty boring."

Language Focus 1 Relative clauses with *who*

1 🎧 **Pair Work** Listen. Then practice this conversation.

A: Interesting people.
B: Yeah, these are the people who worked with me last year.
A: Who is that?
B: That's the guy who hired me.
A: Oh, yeah. That great job you had last year. And who is this?
B: That's the woman who fired me.

2 Complete the definitions. Make statements like this:

"We call someone who .... a ...."

What do you call someone who . . .
a talks a lot about trivial subjects? ....
b talks about other people? ....
c works at the front desk of an office? ....
d has an answer for everything? ....
e plans buildings? ....

3 Combine these sentences using *who*.

Example: Teresa runs the finance department. She is a tough boss.
Teresa, who runs the finance department, is a tough boss.

a Jane works at the front desk. She is a know-it-all.
b Scott brings around the paychecks. He is a nice guy.
c Len delivers the mail. He is a gossip.
d Marcella does word processing. She knows everyone's good and bad points.

4 a Imagine you work in Marcella's office. What would she say about you? Complete the statement.

"Oh, ... He/she is the person who ...."

b **Group Work** Discussion. Compare responses. Who has the most interesting statement? The most unusual? The most accurate?

"I'm thinking of someone who always comes to class early."

5 **Group Work** Take turns thinking of someone in the class. Make up sentences following the model at left and see if your classmates can guess who you are thinking of.

Task 1

a **Pair Work** Which of these words can be used to describe people? Circle them.

meaningful   unlucky   satisfaction   unhappy   boring
frustration   interesting   irritation   satisfying

b Change the other words into words that *can* describe people.

Task 2

a **Pair Work** Evaluate these reasons people gave for working by putting a number (1–5) in each blank. (5 = very important; 1 = unimportant.)

.... People expect you to work. Without a job you're nothing.
.... I work to give my life meaning. No job, no meaning!
.... I took a job to get away from my parents.
.... My job gives me freedom to be creative.
.... I work to support my family.
.... I like to meet people, and I can do that through my work.
.... I'm well educated—I work to use my education.
.... I like excitement, and my job's really exciting.
.... Why do I work? That's easy—to make money.

b **Group Work** Compare your results with another pair's results.

Task 3

a Listen to these people discussing their attitudes toward work and fill in the chart.

NAME	LIKES	DISLIKES
Dennis		
Darlene		
Tom		
Tania		
Peter		

b **Group Work** Discussion. Listen again. What job do you think each of these people does?

c What aspects of a job would be important for each of these people?

1 someone who has a young family
2 someone who likes to travel
3 someone who likes excitement
4 someone who wants to get rich

Task 4

a PairWork Skim the newspaper article below and select an appropriate heading. Check [√] your answer.

☐ Changing Attitudes to Employment
☐ Annual Race for Jobs
☐ Downturn in Economy Reflected in Job Market

b GroupWork Discussion. Which country do you think the author is writing about? What helped you decide? Is this situation similar to your country?

"One advantage of lifelong employment is job security. A possible disadvantage is lack of career opportunities."

This fall, as usual, companies and corporations are busily hiring new graduates. Major cities are crowded with young men and women who have just graduated from high school or college and who are hunting for a job.

"It's really tough," says one recent accounting graduate. "You put on a suit for the first time and run from one interview to another. I had six in one day, and I was one of the lucky ones. Some of my friends didn't get a single interview."

One high school graduate argues that the employment season represents judgment day for many students. "Our whole lives are decided during this period when we're looking for a company to work for," she says. "I know that when I finally land a job, I'll probably be with that company for the rest of my life, and that makes the job search very important."

For some employers, the policy of lifetime employment is particularly important because it means that they can put money and effort into training their staff. The personnel manager of one large firm reports that the policy here is different from most other countries, where companies employ people who are already trained and whose skills can be used immediately. "What we do here, however, is to select young people who have potential and who can be trained," he said. "We then give them the kinds of skills that will make them suitable employees for us. In other words, we tailor the training very much to our particular needs."

One recently employed graduate says that she is receiving a great deal of valuable training from the company. "This means that I will be a loyal employee," she says. "And it also means that the company will want to keep me. I am an important investment for them. So the policy is a good one because it benefits both the employer and the employee."

Recently, however, attitudes toward lifelong employment are beginning to change. Employees are slowly beginning to accept the idea that lifelong employment is not always in their best interest and that changing firms can have career advantages. Companies are also developing more flexible employment policies. "I thought I had a job for life," says one young woman who lasted just six months in her first job. "However, when the company lost a big international order, I was laid off. I'm now looking for another job."

Task 5

a PairWork Look at the article again, and find the advantages and disadvantages of lifelong employment.

b PairWork What is your attitude toward lifelong employment? List the advantages and disadvantages of working for one firm all your life.

Advantages   Disadvantages

c GroupWork Compare your lists with those of another pair.

Task 6

You choose: Do **A** or **B**.

A GroupWork Discussion. Talk about your own job. What do you like? What do you dislike?

B GroupWork Discussion. Think of a job you would all like to do. Brainstorm and make a list of all the advantages and disadvantages of the job. Do you still think that it would be a good job?

Language Focus 2 Adjectives ending in *ed* and *ing*

1 Underline the correct word.

a I guess Nancy was <u>horrified</u>/horrifying at losing her job.
b Did you hear about the horrified/<u>horrifying</u> accident at work?
c I was disappointed/disappointing not to get the job.
d Everyone was surprised/surprising when Tony got fired.
e My job is exhausted/exhausting.
f The job in Mexico should be satisfied/satisfying.
g Aren't you confused/confusing having two jobs?
h Doing the same thing every day is depressed/depressing.

2 Complete these statements using the correct form of the word in italics.

a *disappoint*   Sally is ....*disappointed*.... with her job.
              Sally's job is ...*disappointing*....... .
b *tire*   My job is really ....
c *amaze*   I was .... when they offered me the job.
d *bore*   I stand at a checkout counter all day. It's really
              ....
e *interest*   They were really .... when they heard
              about my job.
f *excite*   We were .... to hear that you got the job.
g *depress*   You work with sick children. Isn't that .... ?
h *fascinate*   She was .... to hear that he was an actor.
i *embarrass*   He was .... to admit that he was
              unemployed.

3 **Pair Work**   Think of jobs to match with these adjectives, and then make
statements following the model.

Example: Being an airline pilot must be a fascinating job.

Adjective	Job
fascinating	*airline pilot*
exciting	....
depressing	....
interesting	....
boring	....
surprising	....
tiring	....

Do you know the rule?

Fill in each blank with one of these phrases: *feelings and attitudes/ persons, actions, or things.*

1 We use the *-ing* form of the adjective to describe

....

2 We use the *-ed* form of the adjective to describe

....

Self-Check

COMMUNICATION CHALLENGE

Look at Challenge 1 on page 111.

1 Write down five new words you learned in this unit.

....

2 Write sentences using three of these new words.

....

....

....

3 Write down three new sentences or questions you learned.

....

....

....

4 Review the language skills you practiced in this unit.
Check [√] your answers.

CAN YOU:

Identify people?　　　　　　□ yes　□ a little　□ not yet
Find or give an example: ....

Discuss pros and cons of jobs?　□ yes　□ a little　□ not yet
Find or give an example: ....

5 Group Work Discussion. Complete this statement and then look on page 11 to check your answer.

"*Making inferences* means ...."

6 Vocabulary check. Check [√] the words you know.

Adjectives				Nouns		Verbs		Wh word
□ amazing	□ disappointed	□ interesting	□ unemployed	□ architect	□ irritation	□ graduate	□ predict	□ who
□ boring	□ disappointing	□ meaningful	□ unhappy	□ athlete	□ know-it-all	□ making	□ support	
□ confused	□ employed	□ satisfied	□ unlucky	□ cashier	□ occupation	inferences	□ would	
□ confusing	□ exciting	□ satisfying		□ employee	□ receptionist	□ mind	□ wouldn't	
□ creative	□ exhausted	□ surprised		□ employer	□ satisfaction			
□ depressed	□ exhausting	□ surprising		□ frustration	□ security			
□ depressing	□ fascinating	□ tiring		□ gossip	□ surgeon			
				□ graduate				

16　The World of Work

2 Making Contact

Warm-Up

Winston: likes the theater
Jim: likes playing tennis
Jean: likes fashion
Grace: likes modern art
Victoria: likes classical music
Carlos: likes travel
Phil: likes parties and dancing
Lily: likes reading and films

Unit Goals

In this unit you will:

Talk about past events

"*I was waiting for the bus when he introduced himself.*"

Give and receive messages

"*Ask Tom to call me when he gets in.*"

A Do you know everyone?

B Who's that over there?

A Oh, that's my housemate.

B He looks friendly.

1 a Look at the eight people pictured here. They are either married or going out with each other. Can you match the couples?

b GroupWork Discussion. What were the reasons for your choices?

2 a PairWork Look at the photograph again and imagine that you share an apartment with one of these people. Think of a quality to describe this person (*interesting, sensitive, intelligent,* etc.) and have a conversation like the one at left.

b PairWork Now change roles and practice the conversation again.

3 a GroupWork Discussion. Read the following paragraph. The main idea is underlined. Why is this the main idea? What is the purpose of the rest of the text (e.g., to explain, define, exemplify)?

<u>If you looked at the results of public opinion surveys, you'd be totally convinced that Americans are "people who need people."</u> 96% of adult Americans said that love and romance is very important in their lives. 86% said that having a "traditional marriage" was a "most important life goal." When asked what they looked for in a relationship, 53% said "love," and 32% said "companionship." When people were asked to list the "great sources of satisfaction" in their lives, more than twice as many people listed "marriage" as listed "friends," "career," or "money."

LEARNING STRATEGY

Discriminating = distinguishing between the main idea and supporting information.

b GroupWork Discussion. Read the text again. Do these statistics surprise you? What are the most important values in your lives?

Task Chain 1 First meeting

Task 1

a What attracts you to people? Rank these qualities from 1 (highest) to 8 (lowest), and write the numbers in column A.

	Column A	Column B	Column C
intelligence	....	....	....
sense of humor	....	....	....
looks	....	....	....
generosity	....	....	....
sensitivity	....	....	....
creativity	....	....	....
knowledge	....	....	....
wealth	....	....	....
other	....	....	....

b Group Work Now ask two other students and complete columns B and C.

c Group Work Discussion. What is the most valued quality in the class? What is the least valued quality?

Task 2

a Group Work Look at the rankings in this chart. Did your choices agree with those of the women who answered the survey?

What Attracts Women to Men?

intelligence	2
sense of humor	6
looks	3
generosity	7
sensitivity	1
creativity	4
knowledge	5
wealth	8

b What do you think the ranking would be if the question was "What attracts men to women?"

Task 3

a 🎧 Listen to Grace talking about meeting her husband. One piece of information in the chart is incorrect. Can you correct it?

NAME	PARTNER	WHERE MET	WHAT DOING	WHAT SAID
Grace	Nick	At home	Sitting on porch	Hi! I'm Nick. You must be Grace.
Victoria				
Phil				
Jean				

"Well, I was watching a soccer game when I met my husband. We had a fight—he said that I was cheering for the wrong team."

b 🎧 Listen to the other conversations (with Victoria, Phil, and Jean) and fill in the rest of the chart on page 18.

c Now look at Warm-Up task 1. Did you guess correctly?

d Imagine you go to the party. Which person would you most like to talk to? Which person would you least like to talk to?

Task 4

Group Work How did you meet your partner, husband/wife, boyfriend/ girlfriend, best friend? Make a list and compare with another group's list. Who had the most interesting or most unusual meeting?

Task 5

a **Group Work** Discussion. A friend writes you the following letter. What's the problem? What advice would you give?

> Dear Sonia,
>
> I'm really sorry you were out when I called. I need some advice and you're the only one I can confide in.
>
> I just got back from Van's party, where I met this stunning woman. It was weird — there was this "thing" between us from the moment we saw each other. We started chatting, and it was amazing how many interests we shared. We have the same tastes in music and art, we like the same movies and the same books. I won't go on.
>
> Anyway... I'd like to ask her out, but I don't know how. You know what a shy guy I am. And I'm not sure if she feels the same about me as I feel about her. Then, of course, there's Lydia. We've been talking about getting married. So you can see what kind of a confused mess I'm in. I'd really appreciate it if you could call me - or write me and give me some advice.
>
> Thanks,
>
> Bill

b **Pair Work** Write a reply with a partner and share it with another pair.

Task 6

Group Work Discussion. What makes the "perfect couple"? What is your "ideal" partner or companion?

Language Focus 1 Past progressive and simple past

1 🎧 **PairWork** Listen, and then practice this conversation.

A: They look like a fun couple.
B: Don't they? They met at my party last year.
A: What happened?
B: Well, he was asking me to dance, and then she came into the room. He took one look at her and forgot all about me.
A: That's too bad.

2 Look at Task Chain 1 and make statements about each person.

a Grace was .... when she met her husband.
b Victoria was .... when she met her husband.
c Phil was .... when he met his wife.
d Carlos was .... when he noticed Jean.

3 Match the sentences and join them with the word *when*.

Example: I was driving to work. The accident happened.
I was driving to work when the accident happened.

a Tony and I were arguing. It started to rain.
b I was going to bed. I fell asleep.
c George and I were playing tennis. Maria told us to keep quiet.
d I was watching TV. Pauline stopped by.

A What were you doing at 7:00 a.m. yesterday?

B I was practicing tai chi.

4 a Write down what you were doing yesterday at these times.

7:00 a.m.	*I was doing yoga.* ....
9:00 a.m.	....
12:30 p.m.	....
3:00 p.m.	....
5:00 p.m.	....
10:30 p.m.	....
12:30 a.m.	....

b **PairWork** Now practice asking and answering questions.

Do you know the rule?

Underline the correct alternative.

We use the past progressive to describe an action in the past that *is completed when another action begins. / is still happening when another action begins.*

5 **PairWork** Complete these statements using a suitable past tense of the verb in brackets. Then practice saying the statements.

a Tina .... [get] married in June.
b I .... [sleep] when the New Year began.
c My family .... [move] to Canada last year.
d My sister and I .... [visit] Mexico last year.
e I .... [live] in the United States this time last year.
f They .... [go] out when the phone rang.

Task 1

a Do you have an answering machine? Have you ever used one? How do you feel about talking to a machine?

b Pair Work Put the following instructions in the correct order.

Answering Machine Instructions

.... After the beep, record your message, speaking clearly and loudly.

.... Then insert the cassette tape and push it down.

.... Here is a sample message: "This is [your name, business, and/or telephone number]. [I am / We are] out right now. To leave a message, speak for up to one minute after the beep. Thank you."

.... Press the recording button again to confirm your message.

.... First, open the cover of the machine.

.... Make sure there is no slack in the tape.

.... Press the recording button until a long beep is heard and then release it.

---

c Pair Work Underline the words that helped you do this task.

d Group Work Compare your responses with another pair's responses.

Task 2

🎧 Listen to the messages and fill in the memos.

Memo To:

From:

Date:

Message:

Taken By:

Memo To:

From:

Date:

Message:

Taken By:

Memo To:

From:

Date:

Message:

Taken By:

Task 3

🎧 Listen to the answering machine messages. Who do you think recorded each message? Write the correct message numbers next to the choices below.

.... a singer   .... a business owner

.... a doctor   .... an actor

Task 4

"Hi, Sarah, this is Jean. Could you ask Tomoko to bring her guitar to class tomorrow? Tell her the rehearsal is immediately after the class."

a **PairWork** Think of someone to call (for example, a friend, relative, classmate, or coworker) and make up a message. Sit back-to-back with your partner and pretend to leave the message on an answering machine. Your partner will make a note of the message and try to guess the reason for the message.

b **GroupWork** Tell another pair about your message for your partner.

c **PairWork** Change roles and do the task again.

Language Focus 2 Requests with *ask* and *tell*

1 🎧 Pair Work Listen, and then practice the conversation.

A: Hello.
B: Hi! This is Tom. Is Sally there?
A: No, she isn't.
B: Oh. Can you ask her to call me?
A: Sure.
B: Tell her that I have a surprise for her.

2 Match these statements and responses and then practice them.

.... Tony is always late for work.
.... Marika won a lot of money last week.
.... I haven't seen Miyoko for ages.
.... John's car broke down again this morning.
.... Donald called while you were out.

a Did you tell him to call back later?
b I'll tell her to call you.
c Tell him to get a new one.
d Tell her not to spend it all at once.
e Tell him to try and leave home earlier.

3 Pair Work Make up some messages using these cues and then practice them.

Example: exam / tomorrow / Sylvia
Please tell Sylvia the exam is tomorrow.

a movie starts / 8:30 / Donna
b I'll be / entrance / 8:15 / the class
c I'll buy / tickets / your friends
d We'll go somewhere / eat after / movie / Alex
e I'll take / home / Cynthia and Tom

4 Make requests using *ask* or *tell*.

Examples: The exam is tomorrow.
Please *tell* Kim the exam is tomorrow.
Pass me the pen.
Could you *ask* Van to pass me the pen?

a Come for dinner tomorrow.
b Tomoko won't be at school today.
c Call me.
d Lend me the book.
e The concert starts at 8:00.

Do you know the rule?

Fill in the blanks with *ask* and *tell*.

When you want someone to pass on a message to a third person, use ....

When you want someone to get a third person to do something, use ....

When passing on advice to a third person, use ....

Self-Check

COMMUNICATION CHALLENGE

Pair Work Student A: Look at Challenge 2A on page 112. Student B: Look at Challenge 2B on page 114.

1 Write down five new words you learned in this unit.

....

2 Write sentences using three of these new words.

....

....

....

3 Write down three new sentences or questions you learned.

....

....

....

4 Review the language skills you practiced in this unit. Check [√] your answers.

CAN YOU:

Talk about past events?   ☐ yes   ☐ a little   ☐ not yet
Find or give an example: ....

Give and receive messages?   ☐ yes   ☐ a little   ☐ not yet
Find or give an example: ....

5 Group Work Discussion. Complete this statement and discuss it.

"*Discriminating* means ...."

6 Vocabulary check. Check [√] the words you know.

Adjectives	Nouns				Verbs		*Wh* words
☐ ideal ☐ perfect	☐ answering	☐ generosity	☐ marriage	☐ romance	☐ argue	☐ pass on	☐ when
☐ intelligent ☐ shy	machine	☐ humor	☐ memo	☐ sensitivity	☐ ask	☐ press	
	☐ companion	☐ intelligence	☐ message	☐ survey	☐ confide	☐ push	
	☐ couple	☐ knowledge	☐ public	☐ wealth	☐ flirt	☐ release	
	☐ creativity	☐ love	opinion		☐ happen	☐ tell	
					☐ introduce		

3 Fifty Years From Now

Warm-Up

Unit Goals

In this unit you will:

Talk about future ability
"In the future, we'll be able to work from home."

Discuss likely and unlikely future events
"If she asks me to help her, I will."
"If they asked me to leave, I would."

1 **Group Work** Look at the picture above and talk about the differences you see between this city of the future and cities of today.

2 a **Pair Work** Match the headings and the TV screens by putting numbers in the blanks.

In the future you will be able to use your TV to . . .

.... order a pizza   .... do your banking   .... see a movie

b **Group Work** Futurologists say we will be able to do all of these things from home. Would you like to be able to do these things from home?

Rank these things from most to least important (1 to 6).

.... do banking
.... order and watch movies
.... order meals
.... turn in school assignments
.... do weekly grocery shopping
.... consult a doctor

1

Worldwide Savings & Loan
How can I help you today?

Select an account:
• Checking Account
• Savings Account
• Money Market Account

2

Videos To Go
Movie Warehouse
• Preview Your Selection
• Browse
• Order
• Help
• Exit

3

Select the Topping(s)
of Your Choice:

Mushrooms   Pepperoni
Eggplant   Onions
Sausage   Peppers
Garlic   Olives

Task Chain 1 Living in the future

"To me, the future means adventure."

Picture ....

Picture ....

Picture ....

Picture ....

Picture ....

Task 1

a GroupWork What does the phrase *the future* mean to you? Brainstorm and think of as many words or phrases as you can.

b GroupWork Compare your ideas with those of another group.

Task 2

a Check [√] the words you know.

- ☐ futurologist
- ☐ computer chip
- ☐ 50 years
- ☐ smart cards
- ☐ scientist
- ☐ order
- ☐ lonely
- ☐ clothes
- ☐ homes
- ☐ movies
- ☐ future
- ☐ food
- ☐ TV/computer
- ☐ household goods
- ☐ entertainment
- ☐ security systems

b You are going to hear a conversation containing the words from Task 2a. What do you think it is about? Check [√] your answers.

	Yes	No	Maybe
Buying goods and services in the future	☐	☐	☐
Being a scientist in the future	☐	☐	☐
The role of technology in the future	☐	☐	☐
Shopping from home	☐	☐	☐

c 🎧 Listen and circle the words in Task 2a when you hear them.

d 🎧 Listen again and number these pictures to match the order in which you hear them being discussed.

e GroupWork Discussion. Look at the phrases in Task 2b and select the one that best matches the conversation.

Task 3

a Look quickly at the magazine article on the following page. What is the information highway?

b How will these things be different in the future as a result of the information highway? Write your answers in the chart.

	NOW	THE FUTURE
News		
Entertainment		
Education		
Health		
Meals		
Groceries		

c GroupWork Discussion. Use the chart to compare life now with life in the future.

Life on the Information Highway

In the town of the future you won't have to spend so much time on the old-style highway—the kind that requires a car. The information highway will let you see and speak to the world without leaving your home. The highway's traffic director will be a telephone or cable company's central office. Your TVs and phones will be linked to this office by a fiber-optic cable. The office will receive video, voice, and data messages and send them out across the country at lightning speed. The office will be your gateway to all sorts of communication services. If you like to watch the news over your morning coffee, plain old cable TV signals will feed into the network from a satellite dish, much as they do today. You will also be able to order your favorite movies whenever you wish from companies that will have thousands stored in computer banks.

Perhaps your child can't get to school. At least he or she can turn in a term paper on time over the fiber-optic cable. Need to pay an account? A link to the local savings and loan will let you write a check on-screen and send it off instantly. Get an electronic examination from the local doctor by placing your arm in a special sensing device. If you end up traveling to the hospital on the old-fashioned kind of road, the doctor there can consult with a specialist at a hospital in a faraway place. They will both be able to look at your results at the same time on their computers, which will be linked together by the information highway. By now you're probably hungry. Technology can only go so far; pizza won't fit through the fiber. But you can see the menu on your TV screen and place an order from your easy chair. While you wait for your food to be delivered, you can do your weekly grocery shopping on the system—the supermarket delivers too. Oh, yes. Work. You'll be able to do that at home too, using your television or computer to see data files instantly and even the smiling faces of your fellow travelers on the information highway.

"I think that the work week will be only two days long."

Task 4

a Which of the following events do you think will happen in the next 50 years? Check [√] your answers.

	Agree	Disagree
1 Scientists will find a cure for AIDS.	☐	☐
2 Smoking will become illegal.	☐	☐
3 Food will be replaced by nutrition pills.	☐	☐
4 The average person will live to be 95.	☐	☐
5 All cars will be powered by electricity.	☐	☐
6 One world government will rule the planet.	☐	☐
7 Humans will make regular trips to the moon.	☐	☐
8 Beings from other planets will visit Earth.	☐	☐

b Group Work Compare responses and discuss any differences.

c Group Work Make a list of predictions about these topics.

Task 5

You choose: Do **A** or **B**.

A Choose one of the topics from Task 3b and write a paragraph about how things will be different in 50 years.

B Group Work Choose one of the topics from Task 3b and give a short talk about how things will be different in 50 years.

Language Focus 1 Modals: *will / won't be able to*

1 Pair Work Listen, and then practice this conversation.

A: What do you think life will be like in twenty years?
B: Well, I think that everyone will be able to work from home.
A: Really? I don't think there will be any work.
B: And I think we'll be able to do our shopping and order food from home.
A: We won't be able to buy real food. We'll all live on pills.
B: And cities will be different. We'll be able to get around on high-speed public transportation.
A: I think that cities will be too big. We won't be able to go anywhere.

2 Complete these statements using the phrases *will be able to* or *won't be able to* and the cues in brackets.

Example: Nancy is taking art lessons, so she ....
[paint picture]
"Nancy is taking art lessons, so she'll be able to paint us a picture soon."

a Susan is taking dancing lessons, so she .... [dance at brother's wedding]
b Tomoko studies really hard, so she .... [go to graduate school]
c Tony never practices his English outside of class, so he .... [pass TOEFL test]
d The Gonzales family is going out of town this weekend, so they .... [come to our party]
e We don't have a car, so we .... [go skiing next weekend]

"I hope I'll be able to speak English much better next year."

3 **a** Make a list of all the things you hope you will be able to do next year that you can't do now.

b Group Work Compare your list with two other students' lists.

4 Group Work Complete this statement and compare it with three other students' statements.

"By the end of this course, I'll be able to ...."

"Will I be able to rent an apartment cheaply?"

5 Pair Work You want to study in North America. Make a list of questions about things such as housing, expenses, part-time work, etc. Ask your teacher about them.

Task Chain 2 Biosphere

jo to the movies! meet me for lunch
what do you do?
why
when neighborhood

LEARNING STRATEGY

Diagramming = using information from a text to label a diagram.

Task 1

a Look quickly at the text below, and then underline the correct choice in these two sentences.

The purpose of the text is to **sell something / give information / tell a story.**

It is part of **a novel / an advertisement / a newspaper article.**

Two years ago, eight adults were locked into a glass "world." Nothing was allowed in or out. The people had to grow their own food and get rid of their own waste products. The builders of Biosphere claim that this is the world of the future. To fund Biosphere, a private company was set up with the financial help of Texas-born billionaire Ed Bass. The company will not reveal the financial details, but Bass's contributions could be as much as $150 million. For many years, Bass has given money to environmental projects, including a rain forest in Puerto Rico and a solar-powered hotel in Katmandu.

Biosphere

Biosphere was set up to help us understand how water, air, soil, plants, and animals interact to keep life going. This understanding can help us preserve the environment here on Earth as well as set up "cities" in space. Scientists argue that without such knowledge the future is bleak.

Biosphere is a huge glass cage built in the middle of the Arizona desert. The structure is made up of 6,488 panes of glass. Inside the sphere are four men and four women, 3,800 plants and animals, an ocean, a desert, a rain forest, and a farm. The humans live in a dome above the sphere. Outside the sphere is a gift shop where visitors can buy souvenirs.

Locking people in a glass cage is a great way to get media publicity, but it hasn't been a complete success. All of the Biosphere inhabitants have lost weight. Insect attacks and disease have ruined many of the crops, and many plants and animals have died. Soon the current crew will pack their bags and head for the outside world. Their place will be taken by a new crew, who will continue the work.

b Read the text again and label the diagram with the words below.

plants   farm   desert   rain forest   dome home   ocean

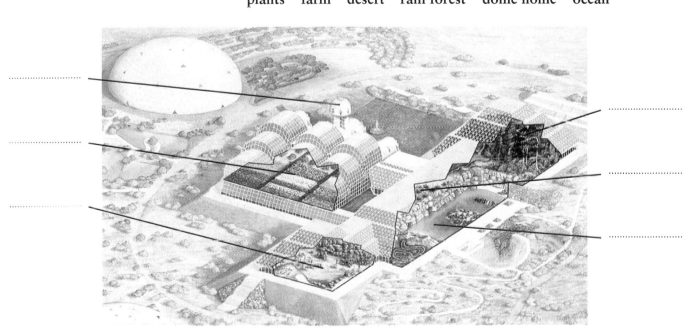

Task 2

a 🎧 Listen to the interview with a new member of the Biosphere crew. Check [√] whether or not the interviewer asks about each topic.

	Yes	No	Not sure
1 leisure activities	☐	☐	☐
2 daily routines	☐	☐	☐
3 food	☐	☐	☐
4 health issues	☐	☐	☐
5 scientific experiments	☐	☐	☐
6 relationships with others	☐	☐	☐
7 boredom	☐	☐	☐
8 concerns of family	☐	☐	☐

b **Pair Work** Compare your responses with those of another student.

c 🎧 Listen again and complete these statements.

1 If the food ran out, ...
2 If I get sick or injured, ...
3 If I got bored, ...
4 If my family wanted me to leave, ...

Task 3

a **Pair Work** Imagine you are going to interview a new member of the Biosphere team. Make a list of questions to ask.

b **Pair Work** Now work with a different partner, and take turns interviewing each other.

Task 4

a Imagine that you have been in the Biosphere for almost two years. Write a letter to a friend or a member of your family telling about your experience. Tell about what you do every day, how you feel, how you spend your leisure time, and what you will do when you get out.

b **Pair Work** Share your letter with another student.

Task 5

a **Pair Work** Imagine you are about to enter the Biosphere for two years. You are only allowed to take five things with you. Make a list of the things you would take.

b **Group Work** Work with another pair, and make up a single list of five items. Give reasons for your choices.

"Well, I'd take a CD player, a box of books, an electronic game, a TV, and a big box of chocolate bars."

Language Focus 2 *If* clauses: future events

1 🎧 PairWork Listen, and then practice the conversation.

A: What will you do if you get bored?
B: That's a possibility. If I get bored, I'll write a book.
A: What will you do if your family wants you to leave?
B: That's not likely. If they wanted me to leave, I guess I'd leave.

2 Read each lettered item and check [√] the sentence that is true.

a If I get bored, I'll write a book.
☐ I probably won't get bored.
☐ I might get bored.

b If they wanted me to leave, I guess I'd leave.
☐ They probably won't want me to leave.
☐ They might want me to leave.

3 Unscramble these words to make three sentences.

have   picnic   our   rains   it   to   cancel   we'll   if
tomorrow   work   million   immediately   I   won   would
I   dollars   a   stop   if   would   exam   think   that   fail
if   an   I   tomorrow   I   had   we

Do you know the rule?

Circle the correct words to complete the statements.

Use *if . . . [verb in present tense] . . . will* to talk about something in the future that is **likely / unlikely**.

Use *if . . . [verb in past tense] . . . would* to talk about something in the future that is **likely / unlikely**.

4 Complete the sentences.

a If I were a scientist, I .... [like] to visit the Biosphere.
b I don't know where the Biosphere is. If I .... [know] where it was, I .... [visit] it.
c If the experiment is a success, scientists .... [build] more "biocities."
d If the inhabitants get sick, they .... [leave].
e I think the experiment will work. It .... [be] a disaster if it .... [fail].

5 PairWork Complete these statements.

a I don't think it'll rain tomorrow, but if it did, I ....
b If I go to Thailand next year, I ....
c If I won a lot of money, I ....
d If I pass the exam, I ....
e If my English improves, I ....
f If I got selected for the Biosphere, I ....

Self-Check

COMMUNICATION CHALLENGE

PairWork Student A: Look at Challenge 3A on page 113. Student B: Look at Challenge 3B on page 115.

1 Write down five new words you learned in this unit.

....

2 Write sentences using three of these new words.

....

....

....

3 Write down three new sentences or questions you learned.

....

....

....

4 Review the language skills you practiced in this unit. Check [√] your answers.

CAN YOU:

Talk about future ability? ☐ yes ☐ a little ☐ not yet

Find or give an example: ....

Discuss likely and unlikely future events? ☐ yes ☐ a little ☐ not yet

Find or give an example: ....

5 GroupWork Discussion. Complete this statement and discuss it.

"*Diagramming* can help us to learn because it ...."

6 Vocabulary check. Check [√] the words you know.

Adjectives	Conjunction	Nouns					Verbs	
☐ environmental	☐ if	☐ ability	☐ cable	☐ future	☐ inhabitant	☐ network	☐ be able to	☐ order
☐ scientific		☐ Biosphere	☐ diagram	☐ futurologist	☐ leisure	☐ satellite	☐ compare	☐ will
☐ solar		☐ boredom	☐ dome				☐ consult	

4 Looking Back

Warm-Up

Unit Goals

In this unit you will:

Report what someone says

"The police said that I was lucky to get out of the accident alive."

Say what people have been doing

"They've been working on the project for months."

1 a Group Work Imagine that you find a time capsule containing the items in the pictures. When do you think it was buried? Check [√] your choice.

Sometime between
☐ 1850 and 1870
☐ 1870 and 1900
☐ 1900 and 1920
☐ 1920 and 1940
☐ 1940 and 1950

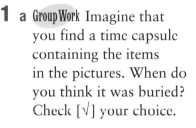

b Group Work Compare your choice with that of another group. Give reasons for your choice.

2 a Group Work What do you think? Which item in each pair has had more impact on humanity? Circle your choices.

1 the printing press or the computer
2 capitalism or communism
3 classical music or pop music
4 electric power or the automobile
5 ships or planes
6 antibiotics or contraceptives
7 heating or refrigeration
8 politicians or athletes
9 gunpowder or nuclear weapons

b Group Work Take a class poll and tabulate the results.

Task 1

a **Pair Work** Look at these newspaper headlines. What do you think that the stories are about? Write your answers in the blanks.

Fifty-Car Pile-up on LA Freeway ....

Forest Ablaze in Santa Cruz ....

Quake Registers 6.6 on Richter Scale ....

b **Group Work** Compare your responses with those of another pair.

Task 2

a Listen to three people talking about something scary that happened to them. Match the incidents with the headlines in Task 1.

INCIDENT	HEADLINE	KEYWORDS
1		
2		
3		

b Listen again. What keywords helped you do Task 2a?

c **Pair Work** Compare your responses with those of another student.

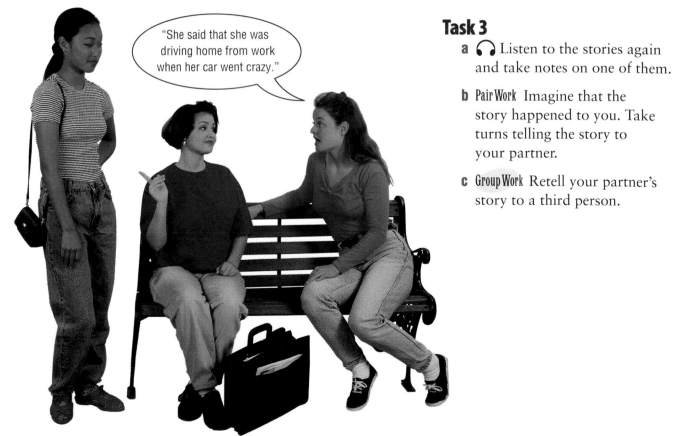

"She said that she was driving home from work when her car went crazy."

Task 3

a Listen to the stories again and take notes on one of them.

b **Pair Work** Imagine that the story happened to you. Take turns telling the story to your partner.

c **Group Work** Retell your partner's story to a third person.

A Do you know what you're doing?

B Of course I know what I'm doing.

Task 4

Rewrite the following story as a dialogue.

"I was walking along the street the other day, and I came across the strangest sight. This guy was standing on the corner tearing up ten-dollar bills. I couldn't help asking him if he knew what he was doing, and he said that of course he knew what he was doing. He was tearing up ten-dollar bills and was throwing them on the ground. So I asked him why he was tearing up the bills, and he replied that it kept the ghosts away. I told him that there were no ghosts, and he said that was because he was tearing up ten-dollar bills."

Task 5

a Think of something scary that happened to you. Make notes about it.

b Pair Work Tell your story to another student.

c Group Work Report your partner's story to another pair. Who has the most unusual or the most interesting story?

Language Focus 1 Reported speech

1 PairWork Take turns reporting what was said.

a "There's a lot of heavy traffic downtown," said the announcer.
The announcer said that *there was a lot of traffic downtown* .

b "The whole city is shaking," said the announcer.
The announcer said that ....

c "Hundreds of people have been killed," said the announcer.
The announcer said that ....

d "They've closed the road," said the announcer.
The announcer said that ....

e "You're lucky to get out alive," said the police officer.
The police officer said that ....

2 a PairWork Your partner tells you the opposite of what he or she told you yesterday. Respond as in the following example.

Example: "I haven't read that book."
"I thought you said you had read it."

1 I haven't seen the new movie at the Regent.
2 Tom and Annie are coming to the party.
3 I'll be late for the meeting tonight.
4 I'm bored with learning English.
5 Tomoko has many new friends.

b PairWork Change roles and practice again.

3 PairWork Report what each person said.

Example: He was in an earthquake once (he told us).
He told us that he had been in an earthquake.

a They were in a bad road accident last year (they reminded us).
b Stella has a scary story to tell (Tony told us).
c My story is too long (they complained).
d We'll have a storytelling competition tomorrow (the teacher promised us).

4 a Add three topics to this list.

playing sports   ....
going to the movies ....
learning English   ....

b GroupWork Take turns asking another student what he or she thinks about the above topics. Report the responses to a third student.

Do you know the rule?

Fill in the blanks.

In reported speech,
are becomes .... ,
am becomes .... ,
is becomes .... ,
have becomes .... ,
and *will* becomes ....

A What do you think about playing sports?

B Oh, I think it's boring.

A Tom said that playing sports was boring.

---

you're invited . . .   go to the movies!   meet me for lunch
what do you do?   why
neighborhood

Task Chain 2 Changing cultures

LEARNING STRATEGY

Using context = using the surrounding text to help you to understand the meaning of unknown words, phrases, and concepts.

Task 1

a PairWork In the following text, the part of the sentence that reads "progress was gradual but inevitable" helps the reader to understand the term *evolution*. Underline those parts of the text that help you to understand the words in bold.

The twentieth century began slowly and seriously. Because of scientific and industrial advances in the nineteenth century, many people believed that the human race was on an inevitable path to perfection. The century of steam was about to give way to the century of oil and electricity, which would be new and important sources of power and light. Charles Darwin's theory of **evolution,** only 41 years old in 1900, proposed a scientific basis for the idea that <u>progress was gradual but inevitable</u>.

No one could have guessed that new ideas would start appearing so frequently that progress would seem to be a race rather than a walk along life's highway. Thrown into this race, the children of the twentieth century would see more changes in their daily lives than had ever before been seen in one generation. This **onslaught,** in which new ideas and technologies poured in on us from every side, for a time seemed to support the older dream that life on Earth was getting better and better all the time.

Every age has ideas and artifacts that **typify** it, that show it to be different from every age that has gone before it. The twentieth century is no exception. In terms of ideas and culture, we have seen the rise of rock music, communism, humanistic psychology, and feminism. In terms of **artifacts,** we have seen the development of high-tech items such as the computer and nuclear medicine as well as low-tech, everyday items such as the ballpoint pen and contact lenses.

b PairWork What do you think was the original title of the article? Check [√] your answer.

☐ Artifacts of the 20th Century
☐ The Astonishing 20th Century
☐ Evolution in the 20th Century

c GroupWork Compare your choice of a title with that of another pair and give reasons for your choice.

Task 2

a GroupWork Discussion. You are going to hear this person talking about his work. What do you think he does? What do you think you will hear?

b 🎧 Listen to the archaeologist talking to a reporter. What are they talking about?

c PairWork Here is part of a newspaper article written by the reporter. The reporter got some things wrong. Can you find them?

> Robert Bolton's first steps into the newly discovered tomb were understandably hesitant. After weeks of digging, during which his team had been working slowly and tediously, they had come across a tomb. Now Dr. Bolton was about to be the first human in a thousand years to enter the ancient tomb. What would he find? A fortune in gold and jewelry? "We expect to find some exciting artifacts," he said. He and his team were not disappointed. Inside were lots of precious jewels as well as ancient clothing. Most interesting to the team, however, was a time capsule. These capsules contain things that ancient people considered to be typical of their societies. Dr. Bolton's team immediately removed the capsule and opened it. Inside was a primitive toothbrush, a spoon, and an early kind of writing instrument. For Dr. Bolton, these everyday objects are more important than the precious jewels because they can help us to understand ourselves as a human race.

d GroupWork Compare your answers with those of another pair.

e 🎧 Listen again to confirm your answers.

Task 3

a Write your own newspaper article about the discovery of the tomb.

b PairWork Compare your version with another student's version.

"How did you feel when you opened the tomb?"

Task 4

PairWork Make a list of questions you would like to ask the archaeologist. Now interview your partner using your questions.

Task 5

You choose: Do **A** or **B**.

A PairWork Brainstorm and decide on ten items to put in a time capsule to give people three hundred years from now an idea of what life was like in our times.

GroupWork Work with another pair. Combine both lists and reduce the 20 items (your ten and the other pair's ten) to one list of ten items.

GroupWork Compare your list with another group's list.

B PairWork Brainstorm and decide on the ten most useful everyday inventions of this century.

GroupWork Work with another pair. Combine both lists and reduce the 20 items (your ten and the other pair's ten) to one list of ten items.

GroupWork Compare your list with another group's list.

Language Focus 2 Present perfect progressive

1 🎧 Pair Work Listen, and then practice the conversation.

A: I haven't seen you at the health club in ages.
B: No, I've been working hard.
A: Why?
B: Well, I have this English exam coming up, so I've been studying hard since the semester began.

2 Pair Work Make questions and answers by following the model.

a The archaeologists started looking for the tomb in January.
It is now August, and they're still looking.
A: *How long have the archaeologists been looking for the tomb?*
B: *They've been looking for the tomb since January.*
  They've been looking for the tomb for seven months.

b The team leader went into the tomb at four o'clock.
It's seven o'clock and he's still in there.
A: ....
B: ....

c The security people started guarding the tomb last night.
It's morning and they're still there.
A: ....
B: ....

d The media started filming half an hour ago.
They're still filming.
A: ....
B: ....

A The head of the archaeology team looks excited.

B Yes, he's been looking for the tomb for five years.

3 a Pair Work Make responses to these statements using the present perfect progressive and the cues provided.

1 The archaeology team looks tired. [work / 6:00 a.m.]
2 They've found a lot of artifacts. [dig / three days]
3 The time capsule looks old. [lie in tomb / thousands of years]
4 The reporter has a great story. [follow team / weeks]
5 The film crew is unhappy. [wait to interview team / eight hours]
6 The interviewer looks bored. [try to talk with archaeologist]

b Group Work Which pair had the most interesting or unusual responses?

Do you know the rule?

Complete the statement.

You can use the present perfect progressive to ....
....

4 Pair Work How many different things can you say about yourself using the following cue? "I've been ...."

5 Pair Work How many questions can you ask your partner using the following cue? "How long .... ?"

Self-Check

COMMUNICATION CHALLENGE

Pair Work Student A: Look at Challenge 4A on page 112. Student B: Look at Challenge 4B on page 114.

1 Write down five new words you learned in this unit.

....

2 Write sentences using three of these new words.

....

....

....

3 Write down three new sentences or questions you learned.

....

....

....

4 Review the language skills you practiced in this unit. Check [√] your answers.

CAN YOU:

Report what someone says? ☐ yes ☐ a little ☐ not yet
Find or give an example: ....

Say what people have been doing? ☐ yes ☐ a little ☐ not yet
Find or give an example: ....

5 Group Work Discussion. Complete this statement and discuss it.

"We can *use context* to help us ...."

6 Vocabulary check. Check [√] the words you know.

Adjectives/Adverbs			Nouns				Verbs	
☐ ancient	☐ gradual	☐ reported	☐ archaeologist	☐ earthquake	☐ nuclear	☐ similarities	☐ choose	☐ report
☐ cellular	☐ high-tech	☐ strangest	☐ capsule	☐ evolution	weapons	☐ technology	☐ collapse	☐ respond
☐ completely	☐ inevitable	☐ terrified	☐ chaos	☐ ghost	☐ overpass	☐ tomb	☐ escape	☐ retell
☐ daily	☐ lucky	☐ understandably	☐ choice	☐ headline	☐ pile-up		☐ glance	☐ shaking
☐ disposable	☐ primitive	☐ unusual	☐ culture	☐ incident	☐ printing		☐ register	
			☐ differences	☐ injury	press			

Task 1

a 🎧 Listen and circle the correct choice.

These people are all talking about their first day at **high school / work / college.**

b 🎧 Listen again and note the words that gave you the clue.

c 🎧 **Pair Work** Listen again, and then complete these statements.

Luciano: I was .... , when ....
Gina: I was .... , when ....
Teresa: I was .... , when ....

d Look at the pictures and identify Luciano, Gina, and Teresa.

"Coming back to Earth Is very strange indeed."

"Sally said that coming back to Earth was very strange indeed."

Task 2

Read the following article and change the direct quotations into reported speech.

Back From the Future

After two years spent living in a glass showcase, scientist Sally Silverstone emerges to tell of her astonishing experience in a world of only eight people.

Sally Silverstone's first steps on Earth were understandably shaky after two years in an alien world. The scientist who emerged from Biosphere II blinking at the sunlight now faces the difficult task of reorienting to the real world. The two-year experiment was intended to prove that a crew could thrive in a sealed, artificial, self contained world. In an exclusive interview, Sally said, "Coming back to Earth is very strange indeed."

"In the sphere, boredom and personality clashes are the major problems. There will always be some arguments, too, but they are generally about what to do next," Sally said. Movies, books, and parties provided relaxation. "Just imagine—there we are having a party with the same eight people every time," Sally said. "I'm able to adapt because I don't like crowds. Now I wonder what it will be like to communicate with more than eight people."

A If I got this job, I would be able to begin work whenever I liked, I'd be able to do a lot of my work from home, and I'd be able to take long vacations.

B I know. You want to be a college professor.

Scene 1

Conversation ....

Scene 2

Conversation ....

Task 3

Group Work Think of the perfect occupation for yourself. Imagine that one day you will work in that occupation. Make up several statements about that occupation that begin like this: "If I got this job, I would ...." The others in the group have to guess the job.

Task 4

a **Pair Work** Listen to two conversations. Then practice this conversation. Use your own words in the blanks.

A: What do you do?
B: I'm a ....
A: That must be ....
B: Yes, it is. But it's also very .... What about you?
A: I'm a ....
B: What's that like?
A: Well, it's .... But it's also ....

b **Pair Work** Change roles and practice the conversation again.

Task 5

a Listen again and match the conversations and the pictures.

b **Pair Work** Have a telephone conversation by following these instructions.

A: (Think of something you want to say to a friend.) Ask if your friend is in.
B: Say that he or she isn't.
A: Ask your partner to take a message.
B: Agree to take the message.
A: Give the message.
B: Repeat the message.
A: Thank your partner and close the conversation.

c **Pair Work** Now change roles and practice again.

6 The Right Thing to Do

Unit Goals

In this unit you will:

Make polite requests
"Could you answer the phone for me?"

Make excuses
"I'm sorry, but I'm busy right now."

Talk about past habits
"I used to watch a lot of TV, but I don't anymore."

Warm-Up

Conversation ....

Conversation ....

1 a Pair Work Look at the pictures. What do you think is happening in each one?

b 🎧 Now listen and match the pictures and conversations.

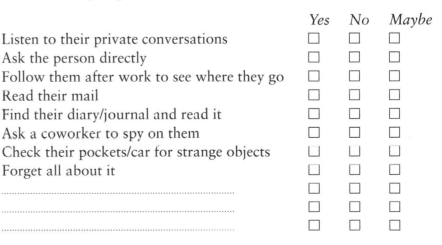

Conversation ....

2 a Someone you know well tells you that he or she thinks their girlfriend or boyfriend is going out with another person. What advice would you give? Check [√] your answers.

	Yes	No	Maybe
Listen to their private conversations	☐	☐	☐
Ask the person directly	☐	☐	☐
Follow them after work to see where they go	☐	☐	☐
Read their mail	☐	☐	☐
Find their diary/journal and read it	☐	☐	☐
Ask a coworker to spy on them	☐	☐	☐
Check their pockets/car for strange objects	☐	☐	☐
Forget all about it	☐	☐	☐
....	☐	☐	☐
....	☐	☐	☐
....	☐	☐	☐

b Pair Work Add three more items to the list and compare your answers with another student's. Give reasons for your answers.

Task Chain 1 Small talk

Task 1

a What kinds of things do you talk about with these people? Fill in the first column below.

> *Example:* "Let's see, with my best female friend, I talk about work, movies, money, sports, other people, books, what to do on the weekend, travel, and families."

b GroupWork Survey. Now ask two other students and fill in the other columns.

What do you talk about with . . .

	YOU	STUDENT 1	STUDENT 2
someone you have just met?			
your best male friend?			
your best female friend?			
your parents?			
your children?			
your teacher?			
your neighbor?			

Task 2

a PairWork Check [√] the words you know. Compare your list with another student's list.

☐ politics ☐ men ☐ marriage ☐ relationships ☐ future plans
☐ vacation ☐ sports ☐ weekend ☐ football team ☐ ourselves

b 🎧 Listen. You will hear three people discussing the things they talk about with their men friends and their women friends. Circle the words when you hear them.

c 🎧 Listen again and summarize what these people say that they talk about.

	With women	*With men*
Hillary		
Stan		

d PairWork Check your responses with those of another student.

Task 3

a Do you talk about different things with male and female friends? Make lists.

b GroupWork Compare your lists with those of three or four other students.

"I talk about the same things with my men friends and my women friends—work, money (usually lack of it!), movies, what's in the news, who's going out with whom."

44 The Right Thing to Do

Task 4

You choose: Read the following extract about differences in men's and women's conversations. Then do **A** or **B**.

In our culture, most people, but especially women, look to their closest relationships as havens in a hostile world. The center of a little girl's social life is her best friend. Girls' friendships are made and maintained by telling secrets. For grown women, too, the essence of friendship is talk, telling each other what they're thinking and feeling, and what happened that day: who was at the bus stop, who called, what they said, how that made them feel. When asked who their best friends are, most women name other women they talk to regularly. When asked the same question, most men will say it's their wives. After that, many men name other men with whom they do things such as play tennis or baseball (but never just sit and talk) or a chum from high school whom they haven't spoken to in a year.

=====

When most men talk to their friends on the phone, they may discuss what's happening in business, the stock market, the soccer match, or politics. They do gossip (although they may not call it that) in the sense of talking about themselves and other people. But they tend to talk about political rather than personal relationships: institutional power, advancement and decline, a proposal that may or may not get through the committee, a plan for making money.

A Pair Work Make notes on the following questions.

1 According to the text, what do women usually talk about?

2 What do men usually talk about?

3 When do differences between men's and women's conversations begin?

4 Do you agree with the author of the text? Why or why not?

5 What are the similarities and differences between the points made here and the discussion of men's and women's conversations in Task 2?

Group Work Compare your responses with those of another pair.

B Write a title for the above article. ....

Pair Work Compare titles and select the one you like best.

Task 5

a Make lists of acceptable and unacceptable small talk (casual conversation) topics in your country.

b Group Work Discuss the kinds of casual conversation topics that are acceptable in your country. Do topics differ in all male, all female, and mixed groups? Can you think of reasons why some topics are acceptable and others are unacceptable?

c Group Work Discussion. What is your attitude toward small talk? Do you enjoy it? Do you find it difficult in a second language?

"Where I come from, the first step in getting to know someone is to find out if the other person is higher or lower than you socially. So you find out a person's age and occupation first. Asking someone's opinion about a topic comes later."

Language Focus 1 Requests with *could*, excuses

1 🎧 Pair Work Listen, and then practice the conversations. Use your own names.

A: Could you lend me that book you were telling me about?
B: No, I'm sorry, I can't. I gave it to a friend.

A: Hello. Could I speak to Jim, please?
B: Speaking.
A: Jim, this is Hillary. I have a doctor's appointment tomorrow, so I won't be at school. Could you tape the class for me?
B: No, I'm sorry, I can't. I have a dentist's appointment, so I won't be at school either.

2 Pair Work What would you say in these situations?

a You have a shirt that needs washing, and you do not have time to do it. Your friend is going to the laundromat.

b The telephone is ringing, and you are in the bathroom.

c You are late for work, and a coworker pulls up in her car.

d You need to borrow some money, and you see a friend coming out of the bank.

Dear Sally,
Could you tape this afternoon's class? I have a doctor's appointment and can't make it.
Suzie

3 a Read the note at left.

b Pretend you're Sally. You're not going to class this afternoon either. Write a note back to Suzie making an excuse. Then write to a third person asking if that person can tape the class.

"I'm sorry, but I'm not going to the lecture either."

4 Pair Work Think of excuses for not carrying out these requests and practice them with another student.

a Could you please tape the lecture this afternoon? I can't make it.
b Could you lend me $50 till tomorrow?
c Could I borrow your car this evening? I need to take a friend out.
d My cousin is visiting town. I'm busy today. Could you show him around?
e I'm going away for a week. Could you collect my mail each day?"

5 a Pick one of the above requests and write a note making the request.

b Pair Work Exchange notes with another student and write a reply, making an excuse for saying no to the request.

jo to the movies!   meet me for lunch
what do you do?   why
neighborhood

Task Chain 2 Eavesdropping

LEARNING STRATEGY

Using a dictionary = finding the spelling, pronunciation, part of speech, meaning, and origin of an unknown word in a dictionary. All of these things can help you remember new words.

eaves (ēvz) *n. pl.* overhanging edge of roof;

eavesdrop *v.i.* to stand under this to listen to secrets; to listen secretly to private conversations;

eavesdropper, one who does this.

From *The Newbury House Dictionary of American English*

Task 1

a Read the article excerpt at right.

b **PairWork** What do you think the word *eavesdrop* means? Check [√] your answer.

- ☐ to take part in someone else's conversation
- ☐ to listen in on someone else's conversation
- ☐ to read someone else's notices and messages

c Look at the dictionary entry at left. How does it explain where the word *eavesdrop* came from?

Human Curiosity

In our day-to-day life we all occasionally *eavesdrop* on other people's conversations or casually look at a friend's kitchen bulletin board. Unfortunately, we're often not even aware that we're doing it.

Task 2

a Would you do any of the following things? Check [√] your choices.

	Yes	No	Not sure
read someone else's private mail	☐	☐	☐
eavesdrop on someone who is talking about you	☐	☐	☐
find out what the boss really thinks of you	☐	☐	☐
listen in on a private telephone conversation	☐	☐	☐
read a friend's diary	☐	☐	☐

b **GroupWork** Compare your responses with those of two other students.

Task 3

a **GroupWork** Read the following article and underline the words you do not understand. Try to guess the meanings.

Office Espionage

The office is a place full of secrets—confidential management plans, colleagues' salaries, what our boss really thinks of us, and, in this day and age, just how secure our job is. Curiosity to know more about what is happening in the office drives many people to office espionage. Here are some examples from a study by Professor Peter Emmett.

- "Several times, I have caught members of my staff going through my planner to see who I was seeing and what I was up to." *Virginia, 36, Financial Service Manager*

- "At home, I'm not at all interested in spying on my girlfriend—I figure what I don't know won't hurt me. But since I've been the manager in our office I go into the fax room and read everybody else's memos." *Stewart, 30, Sales Manager*

- "I was standing by the computer printer one day waiting for a document. Suddenly it started to print something else. I took a look and noticed that it was from my boss. It was his application for another job. After I read it, I took it and put it on his desk. He didn't say anything, but he looked very embarrassed. And I know he didn't get the job because he's still my boss." *Katrina, 28, Legal Secretary*

b Now find the words in your dictionary.

c GroupWork Discussion. How did the dictionary help you increase your understanding of unknown words? Did the words you looked up have more than one meaning? How did you know which one was the appropriate one?

Task 4

a 🎧 Listen to the conversation. What did Professor Emmett find? Check [√] your answers.

Most people would like to . . .	*Yes*	*No*	*Not sure*
1 rob a bank	☐	☐	☐
2 find out about other people by looking at their personal possessions	☐	☐	☐
3 eavesdrop when someone else is talking about them	☐	☐	☐

Some people would like to . . .			
4 find out as much as they can about their spouse/girlfriend/boyfriend	☐	☐	☐
5 listen to private telephone conversations	☐	☐	☐
6 read their partners' letters	☐	☐	☐
7 read their partners' diaries	☐	☐	☐

b 🎧 Listen again and look at the pictures at the beginning of the unit. Which of these people took part in the professor's study?

Task 5

a GroupWork Discussion. What would you say in these situations?

1 You catch someone at work/school going through your diary.

2 You catch your boss in the fax room reading everyone else's private messages.

3 Your boss catches you reading his application for a job as it comes off the office printer.

b PairWork Now role-play one of the situations with another student.

"Excuse me, but I believe that diary belongs to me."

go to the movies!   meet me for lunch
what do you do?   why
neighborhood

Language Focus 2 *Used to*

1 Change these sentences using the phrase *used to*.

Example: "When I was a kid I watched a lot of TV, but I don't anymore."
"I used to watch a lot of TV."

a When I was younger, I eavesdropped on other people's private conversations, but I don't anymore.
b There were lots of eavesdroppers around our office, but there aren't anymore.
c My sister read her boyfriend's diary, but she doesn't anymore.
d Our neighbor had two wives, but now he has none.
e I was curious about other people's private lives, but I'm not anymore.
f My sister was in love with two different guys, but now she isn't in love with anyone.

2 a 🎧 Listen. You will hear someone talk about their past bad habits. Make notes of what you hear using the phrases *used to* and *never used to*.

— used to watch
movies all the time
— never used to
study

b Pair Work Take turns saying what the person did and didn't do.

"I used to play tennis, but I don't anymore."

3 Pair Work Make statements using these cues and practice them. Then add some cues of your own and have your partner make statements.

a eat	**d** go to	**g** ....
b listen to	**e** read	**h** ....
c watch	**f** study	**i** ....

4 a Pair Work Ask and answer questions about games, hobbies, books, movies, and TV.

Example: "What did you use to watch on TV when you were a child?"
"I used to watch *Sesame Street*."

b Group Work Find another pair and tell them about your partner.

Example: "Yani used to watch *Sesame Street* on TV, but he doesn't anymore."

Self-Check

**COMMUNICATION
CHALLENGE**

Pair Work Student A:
Look at Challenge 6A
on page 116. Student B:
Look at Challenge 6B
on page 118.

1 Write down five new words you learned in this unit.

....

2 Write sentences using three of these new words.

....

....

....

3 Write down three new sentences or questions you learned.

....

....

....

4 Review the language skills you practiced in this unit.
Check [√] your answers.

CAN YOU:

Make polite requests?　　　　□ yes　　□ a little　　□ not yet

Find or give an example: ....

Make excuses?　　　　　　　□ yes　　□ a little　　□ not yet

Find or give an example: ....

Talk about past habits?　　　□ yes　　□ a little　　□ not yet

Find or give an example: ....

5 *Group Work* Discussion. How can *using a dictionary* help us be better
language learners and users?

6 Vocabulary check. Check [√] the words you know.

Adjectives/Adverbs			Nouns			Verbs		
□ anymore	□ embarrassed	□ private	□ appointment	□ espionage	□ request	□ check	□ form	□ socialize
□ casual	□ grown	□ wild	□ calendar	□ excuse	□ research	□ could	□ gossip	□ spy
□ confidential	□ hidden		□ curiosity	□ planner	□ small talk	□ eavesdrop	□ realize	□ understand
□ curious	□ polite		□ diary	□ relationship	□ trouble	□ follow	□ select	□ used to

7 Customs

Warm-Up

Picture 1   Picture 2   Picture 3

Unit Goals

In this unit you will:

Tell a story about something that happened to you

"I sat down, and I knew I had done something wrong. . . ."

Discuss your attitudes toward past events

"You should have left a larger tip."

Express regret

"I should have called her earlier."

1 a GroupWork Discussion. Look at the pictures. Do you think that these people are good friends or people who work together? Give reasons.

b GroupWork Brainstorm. Make a list of the possible problems that a foreigner might have eating out with business acquaintances in your country. Compare these with three other students.

2 a Have you ever lived in a foreign country? How did you feel?

b Here are words associated with living in another culture. Check [√] the expressions you know and look up the others in a dictionary.

☐ culture shock   ☐ interesting   ☐ unusual   ☐ exciting
☐ confusing   ☐ tiring   ☐ depressing ☐ strange
☐ fascinating   ☐ homesick   ☐ difficult ☐ boring

c Classify the words by putting them in the chart.

POSITIVE	NEGATIVE	NEUTRAL

A I think it would be exciting to live in another country because I'd get to meet new and different people and learn another language.

B Well, I think I'd have culture shock.

d GroupWork Make statements about living in another country.

Task Chain 1 An embarrassing incident

Picture 1

Picture 2

Picture 3

Picture 4

Picture 5

Picture 6

Picture 7

"Well, I think she's Amy, because she looks like she has a sense of humor."

Task 1

a **Pair Work** You are going to hear three people talking about three embarrassing incidents. Here are some of the words you will hear in each story. Can you tell where each incident took place?

Incident #1: **lunch   salespeople   plastic food   tray   tapped   cheesecake   broke off   smeared   counter   embarrassed**
Where: ....

Incident #2: **grade   gym   girls   boys   swinging   running   track   jumped   swing   shorts   ripped   cover up**
Where: ....

Incident #3: **Taiwan   least important person   manager   Asian office   sales representative   seat   uncomfortable   something wrong**
Where: ....

b 🎧 Listen. Were your predictions correct? Which story was the easiest to predict? Which one was the most difficult to predict?

Task 2

a 🎧 Listen again. Write down each person's embarrassing moment.

Person # 1 (Moses)   ....
Person # 2 (Amy)   ....
Person # 3 (Eric)   ....

b Who said this?

"We had finished doing our running around the track."   ....
"I could tell somehow I had done something wrong."   ....
"We had eaten, and we were leaving the restaurant."   ....

Task 3

Group Work Discussion. Look at these photographs. Which do you think is Moses? Amy? Eric? Can you give a reason for your choices?

Task 4

a 🎧 Listen to Amy and Eric talking further about his embarrassing incident. What had he done wrong?

b **Group Work** Discussion. Look at the pictures at the beginning of the unit. Which one shows Eric's embarrassing incident? Give reasons for your choice.

c Write a letter from Eric to his wife, telling what happened. Begin like this:

> Dear Molly,
> A really embarrassing thing happened to me last night.
> I went out to dinner with the manager of our Asian office and some other important people, and . . . .
> Love, Eric

Task 5

a List three things a foreigner visiting your country should do and five things they should not do.

b **Pair Work** Now talk with another student and compare your lists.

Should do   Shouldn't do

A Well, in my country, you shouldn't shake hands when you first meet someone.

B Interesting. In my country, you should never tip.

LEARNING STRATEGY

Concept mapping = showing the main ideas in a text in groups that form a "concept map."

Task 6

Read the following text and complete the concept map by putting words in the spaces provided in the map.

Living and working in another country can have many advantages. Finding out about other people can be exciting, learning another language can be very rewarding, and getting to know a new culture can be extremely interesting. But there are disadvantages. Many people living abroad go through periods of culture shock. People with culture shock feel homesick and depressed at being away from their family and friends. Unfamiliar customs can be confusing, leading to embarrassing incidents. Furthermore, finding somewhere to live can be difficult.

Living In Another Country

	Advantages			Disadvantages	
people	....	culture	culture shock	....	accommodations
....	rewarding	....	....	confusing, embarrassing	....

Task 7

Group Work Discussion. Use the concept map to discuss the advantages and disadvantages of living in another country. What would/do you like best about living abroad? What would/do you miss most?

Language Focus 1 Past perfect

1 a Number these sentences to tell a story.

.... After I had eaten, I asked my friend why everyone was looking and laughing.

.... I went to a restaurant with a Korean friend and ordered a bowl of noodles.

.... While I was eating, everyone was looking at me and some people started laughing.

.... An embarrassing thing happened to me in Korea.

.... She said it was because I had picked up the chopsticks the wrong way and was holding them too close to the bottom.

b Underline the simple past tense and circle the past perfect tense in the sentences above. (An example of each has been done for you.)

c Pair Work Now tell the story in your own words.

"By the time I arrived at the restaurant, Eric had already left."

"I went to the party after I had completed my assignment."

2 Pair Work Make statements using the information in the two columns. The first two statements have been done for you at left.

Time before point in past	*Time at point in past*
a Eric leaves the restaurant.	I arrive at the restaurant.
b I complete my assignment.	I go to a party.
c Alice accepts a party invitation.	I invite Alice to dinner.
d Tomoko goes out.	We visit Tomoko.
e Nadia does research in library.	Nadia writes her assignment.
f Paul finishes his exams.	Paul takes a vacation.

Do you know the rule?

True or false?

T / F The past perfect describes something that is happening at a past point in time.

T / F The past perfect describes something that happened before a past point in time.

3 Pair Work Talk about an embarrassing incident that has happened to you. Start your conversation like this:

A: Has anything embarrassing ever happened to you?
B: Yes, it has.
A: Really? What happened?
B: Well, I had just .... when ....

Task Chain 2 Tipping

tip /tĭp/, *n.* 1. a slender or pointed extremity, especially of anything long and tapered: *the tips of the fingers.*
2. the top, summit, or apex.
3. a small piece or part, as of metal or leather, forming the extremity of something.
4. a small present of money given to someone, as a waiter, porter, etc., for performing a service.
5. a useful hint or idea.

From *The Newbury House Dictionary of American English*

Task 1

In this chain, we look at the custom of tipping. Look at the dictionary definitions at left. Which one do you think defines *tipping* as we are going to use it in this unit?

Task 2

Pair Work You are going to hear people talking about tipping in restaurants in different countries. Do you know if people tip in restaurants in these countries? Check [√] your answers.

	Yes	No	Not sure		Yes	No	Not sure
Italy	☐	☐	☐	Australia	☐	☐	☐
United States	☐	☐	☐	Singapore	☐	☐	☐
Great Britain	☐	☐	☐	Brazil	☐	☐	☐
Japan	☐	☐	☐				

Task 3

a 🎧 Listen and check [√] these expressions when you hear them.

☐ I find tipping very difficult and embarrassing.
☐ She didn't leave a big enough tip.
☐ I'm pretty careful to give people their 15% unless I really dislike the service.
☐ My attitude's changed a lot since living in the States for seven years.
☐ I hate going out with my British friends, because they don't tip enough.
☐ We do not encourage tipping.

b 🎧 Listen again. Draw lines to match the countries and the comments.

Country	Comment
▪ United States	▪ You have to tip everywhere you go.
▪ Australia	▪ There's no tipping of any kind.
▪ Italy	▪ Tipping is not a big feature of daily life.
▪ Brazil	▪ Tipping's part of the culture.
▪ Singapore	▪ It depends on the person.
▪ Britain	▪ We do not encourage tipping.
▪ Japan	▪ Waiters have to rely on tips to make a reasonable income.

c What do these people think of tipping? Listen and note keywords.

Peter: ....

Liz: ....

Pauline: ....

d GroupWork Discussion. Is the conversation based more on fact or more on opinion?

Task 4

a Complete this survey.

b GroupWork Now compare your responses with those of three or four other students.

Tipping: How Do You Really Feel?

Whom should you tip? How much? Do they really deserve it? Do you wish more countries discouraged tipping?

Do you like to decide the tip, or do you prefer a preset charge?

☐ Preset service charge   ☐ Tip

Is there anyone you just hate to tip?

☐ Waiter   ☐ Taxi driver   ☐ Tour guide
☐ Room service   ☐ Bellhop   ☐ Other ....
☐ Housekeeper   ☐ Hairdresser

What's the biggest tip you've given? What were the circumstances?

....

....

What rule do you follow when you don't know how much to tip?

....

....

Task 5

You choose: Do **A** or **B**.

A PairWork Role-play. You are talking to people who are about to visit your country. Your partner can be one of the visitors. Tell them about tipping. Do they have to tip? How much should they tip? What might happen if they tip the wrong amount?

PairWork Now change roles and listen to your partner talking about tipping.

B PairWork What do you think of tipping? Do you think it's a good thing, a bad thing, or are you neutral? How much do you think people should be tipped?

Language Focus 2 Past modal: *should have/shouldn't have*

1 🎧 **Pair Work** Listen and then practice this conversation.

A: Are you ready for the exam today?
B: No, I'm not. I should have stayed home last night and studied.
A: What did you do?
B: I went to the rock concert at the Stadium.
A: You shouldn't have done that.
B: No, and I shouldn't have gone to the party afterward, either.

2 a Complete these conversations by using the cues in brackets and the phrases *should have* and *shouldn't have*.

1 A: Why are you wet?
   B: I was waiting for the bus, and it started to rain.
   A: I'm sorry.
   B: *Well, I should have taken an umbrella* . [take umbrella]

2 A: Did you see Teresa yesterday?
   B: No, I was supposed to meet her, but I didn't have time.
   A: That's too bad!
   B: .... [call her]

3 A: Why are you late?
   B: I caught a taxi, and I got stuck in traffic.
   A: That's too bad.
   B: .... [take subway]

4 A: How did you do on the exam?
   B: Not very well.
   A: Why?
   B: Well, I was going to study last night, but Bobbie called and invited me to a movie.
   A: And you went?
   B: .... [not go out]

5 A: Did you buy anything for Yumiko?
   B: No, I didn't. Why?
   A: It's her birthday.
   B: .... [remember]

b **Pair Work** Now practice the conversations.

A I should have apologized to my boyfriend for being late.

B And I shouldn't have stayed out so late last night.

3 a **Group Work** Make a statement about something you should have or shouldn't have done.

b **Group Work** Compare your statements with those of another group. Which group has the most interesting statements?

Self-Check

COMMUNICATION CHALLENGE

Look at Challenge 7 on page 117.

1 Write down five new words you learned in this unit.

....

2 Write sentences using three of these new words.

....

....

....

3 Write down three new sentences or questions you learned.

....

....

....

4 Review the language skills you practiced in this unit.
Check [√] your answers.

CAN YOU:

Tell a story about something that happened to you? □ yes □ a little □ not yet

Find or give an example: ....

Discuss your attitudes toward past events? □ yes □ a little □ not yet

Find or give an example: ....

Express regret? □ yes □ a little □ not yet

Find or give an example: ....

5 GroupWork Discussion. Complete the following statement.

"Concept mapping involves ...."

6 Vocabulary check. Check [√] the words you know.

Adjectives/Adverbs

□ comparatively	□ flexible	□ homesick	□ strange
□ difficult	□ frequently	□ immediately	□ uncomfortable
□ embarrassing	□ hollow	□ reasonable	

Nouns

□ acquaintance	□ culture	□ noodles
□ attitude	shock	□ regret
□ cheesecake	□ customs	□ representative
□ chopsticks	□ gym	□ shorts
	□ income	□ tip
	□ map	

Verbs

□ accept	□ should
□ break off	□ shouldn't
□ decline	□ smear
□ invite	□ tip
□ rip	

8 Relationships

Warm-Up

Picture 1   Picture 2   Picture 3

Unit Goals

In this unit you will:

Talk about personal qualities

"I can't stand selfish people."

Give reasons

"I forgot to buy a present, so I didn't go to the wedding."

"I didn't go to the wedding because I forgot to buy a present."

"I think that a sense of humor is the most important because it keeps people from taking themselves too seriously."

1 GroupWork Discussion. Look at the pictures. Is there anything interesting or unusual about any of them? Which wedding group would you like to meet? Why? Can you guess which countries these people come from?

2 a The following questions are supposed to show whether a relationship will last. Rank them from most to least important (1 to 6).

.... Do you share the same view of the world?
.... Do you have the same sense of humor?
.... Does he/she like your friends and family?
.... Is he/she really listening to you?
.... Do you share the same views about money?
.... Does he/she fight fair?

b GroupWork Discuss your rankings. Give reasons for your choices.

c GroupWork Think of three other questions.

.... ?
.... ?
.... ?

d GroupWork Compare your questions with another group's questions.

Task Chain 1 He's really boring

Task 1

a Check [√] the words you know. Look up the others in your dictionary.

☐ ambitious   ☐ loving   ☐ kind   ☐ interesting   ☐ jealous
☐ aggressive   ☐ boring   ☐ sexy   ☐ energetic   ☐ loyal

b **Group Work** Discussion. Which of these words do you think that people would use to describe you?

Task 2

🎧 **Pair Work** Listen and identify the personal qualities you hear. Write them in the first column.

QUALITIES	VERY / REALLY	KIND OF / SORT OF	NOT AT ALL

"Well, I'd say I'm very kind, not at all interesting or aggressive, extremely loyal, somewhat jealous at times, not at all ambitious or angry, but kind of selfish in some ways."

Task 3

🎧 Now listen to Linda, Joseph, and Selina talking about themselves, and write their names in the appropriate boxes in the chart.

Task 4

Group Work Work with two other students. Talk about your own qualities, and write your name in the correct boxes in the chart.

Task 5

a Scan the following magazine article and underline the personal qualities. The first one has been done for you.

Personal qualities generally have either positive or negative connotations. Our attitudes toward such personal qualities are partly personal, partly social, and partly cultural. Some people also feel that gender plays a role, with some qualities being more positively valued by women than by men and vice versa. Such attitudes are not always static, and they can change with changing economic and social circumstances. In some places, during the 1970s, <u>ambition</u> was seen to be bad, and then, during the 1980s, it was seen to be good. During the harsh economic times of the early 1990s, a high value was placed on generosity and compassion.

Despite personal, cultural, and gender differences, there are some qualities that seem to be highly regarded in many different societies and cultures. For example, most people place a high positive value on qualities such as loyalty, kindness, and humor, and a negative value on anger and greed. Our personal reaction toward these qualities is probably conditioned by how we would like others to act toward us. Most of us would like other people to treat us with kindness and compassion, not with aggressiveness or anger.

In cross-cultural terms, there are some qualities, such as generosity, that are highly regarded in many different cultures, while others, such as hatred, that are seen as negative. However, other qualities, such as aggression, might be highly valued in some cultures and not in others. For example, in the United States individual competitiveness is highly valued (although this is beginning to change with an increasing focus on teamwork). In many Asian cultures, the focus is on group consensus, and individual competitiveness is sometimes frowned upon.

b Pair Work Read the text again and find the main idea. Make up a title that reflects the main point. ....

c Group Work Compare your title with the titles created by two other pairs.

Task 6

a Group Work Brainstorm with three or four other students and make lists of the personal qualities that you value highly and the qualities you feel are most negative.

Positive

....
....
....
....
....

Negative

....
....
....
....
....

b Group Work Compare your lists with another group's lists.

Language Focus 1 — Adjectives and nouns

1 🎧 **PairWork** Listen. Then practice the conversation.

A: What kind of things do you look for in a woman?

B: Oh, I guess someone who's kind. Yes, definitely kindness. And she has to be interesting—someone who has an interesting job or has had interesting experiences. How about you?

A: Oh, I'd look for someone who's ambitious, first of all.

B: Really?

A: Sure, why not? She definitely should have ambition. And then I also think that she should be loyal. Loyalty is one thing I'd insist on.

B: What about negative qualities, things that turn you off?

A: Jealousy, I guess. My last girlfriend was jealous, and it drove me crazy. Jealousy and aggressiveness. How about you?

B: Oh, selfishness—definitely. I can't stand selfish people. And anger. I don't like people who are angry a lot of the time.

2 Underline the adjectives and circle the nouns in the above conversation and then complete the chart.

ADJECTIVES	NOUNS
kind	kindness
interesting	

Face 1

Face 2

Face 3

Face 4

Face 5

3 **GroupWork** Take turns making statements about other members of the class, and see if they can guess who you are describing.

4 **GroupWork** Look closely at the illustrations at left. What expressions do you see on the faces?

5 a Fill in the blanks with an appropriate adjective or noun.

I'm a very .... person. I'm .... and I have a lot of .... My friends say that I'm .... and that I can be .... On the other hand, I have .... I tend to be a bit .... My friends say the best thing about me is that I'm not very ....

b **PairWork** Now talk about yourself with your partner.

Task Chain 2 A beautiful wedding

Task 1

a 🎧 Listen to three different people talking about their weddings. Which words do you hear in each conversation? Check [√] in the correct columns.

	Wedding 1	*Wedding 2*	*Wedding 3*
married	☐	☐	☐
marriage	☐	☐	☐
wedding	☐	☐	☐
husband	☐	☐	☐
wife	☐	☐	☐
bride	☐	☐	☐
family	☐	☐	☐
relatives	☐	☐	☐
ceremony	☐	☐	☐
dance	☐	☐	☐
party	☐	☐	☐
ring	☐	☐	☐

b 🎧 PairWork Compare your responses with those of another student, and then listen again to confirm your responses.

Task 2

a GroupWork Draw lines to match the weddings with the unusual events.

Wedding 1	guests pinned money on the couple
Wedding 2	had three weddings
Wedding 3	bride forgot the ring

b 🎧 Listen again to confirm your choices.

c Now look at the pictures at the beginning of the unit and identify the people you heard speaking.

Task 3

a Scan the paragraphs from the newspaper article on page 64 and decide on the best order for the paragraphs. Number the paragraphs from 1 to 4.

.... Others did not see it that way. They feared that just the opposite message would be conveyed. The fact that Ms. Owada gave up her career in order to marry the crown prince was a cause of great concern. These people felt that the marriage of the witty, well-educated career diplomat would send a negative message to other Japanese women—the message that even in these liberated times, women are expected to give up their careers and education for the sake of a husband and family.

.... People in Japan talked of nothing else for months, and the romance between the prince and the diplomat was extremely popular among most sections of Japanese society. However, it did cause confusion and controversy in one sector of society—the Japanese women's movement.

.... On the one hand, some feminists were very happy that a serious, highly educated and qualified career woman was chosen, rather than the traditional royal bride: an obedient, gentle, and quiet woman, offering qualities no more ambitious than the abilities to compose poetry, arrange flowers, and raise children. They felt that at last the rights of women were being recognized and that where the royal family had ventured, other sectors of society would inevitably follow. They also felt that, while she was giving up her diplomatic career, she was embracing a more significant one.

.... In 1993, there was a royal wedding in Japan. Masako Owada, a commoner, married Crown Prince Naruhito. The ceremony was one of the wedding events of the decade. The choice of Ms. Owada as a royal bride captured the interest and imagination of people around the world. Not only was she a commoner, but she was highly educated, spoke several languages, had been educated in the United States, and had an excellent career in the diplomatic service. Her decision to accept the prince's offer of marriage therefore marked a major change in Japanese royal tradition.

LEARNING STRATEGY

Summarizing = picking out and presenting the major points in a text.

b GroupWork Discussion. Which words and phrases helped you to put the paragraphs in order?

c Summarize the arguments for and against the prince's choice of a bride.

For: ....

Against: ....

d GroupWork Discussion. What do you think? Do you believe that Masako Owada took on a more important career or not?

Task 4

You choose: Do **A** or **B**

A What kinds of special events are celebrated in your country—for example, weddings, births, religious festivals, sporting events? Make a list and rank these from least to most important.

PairWork Compare your list with another student's list.

B In the second wedding in Tasks 1 and 2, all the males who danced with the bride pinned money on her dress. This is a custom in some cultures. Make a list of wedding customs in your country.

PairWork Compare your customs with those of another student.

Language Focus 2 Clauses of reason with *so* and *because*

1 🎧 **Pair Work** Listen. Then practice the conversation.

A: I didn't see you at Anita and Paul's wedding.
B: No, I wasn't there.
A: Why not?
B: Well, I forgot to buy them a present, so I didn't go.
A: You were embarrassed?
B: Right.
A: To be honest, I didn't really want to go. I only went because Anita is my sister's best friend.

2 Match the two halves of the sentences using the words *because* or *so*. Write the correct words in the first set of blanks and then write the correct letters to match the sentence parts.

a And for this dance you have to pay the bride, ...
b We wanted a cheap wedding, ...
c A lot of the Turkish family wasn't able to come, ...
d We wanted only close friends and family, ...
e My sister got married at Christmas, ...

.... we were poor students when we got married.
.... when we were in Istanbul we had another wedding there.
.... various members of the family were visiting at the time.
.... we had a small wedding.
.... we ended up with a lot of money on our wedding night.

3 Combine these statements using either *so* or *because*.

Examples: I didn't go to the wedding. I forgot to buy a present.
"I forgot to buy a present, so I didn't go to the wedding."
"I didn't go to the wedding, because I forgot to buy a present."

a My friend got married in Acapulco. His wife is Mexican.
b His family couldn't go to Acapulco. He got married again in Boston.
c His family is unhappy. He's going to live in Mexico City.
d He couldn't come to our farewell party. He left for Mexico last week.

4 **Group Work** Think of three things you did or didn't do recently, and give reasons. Follow this model.

"I didn't .... , so I ...."

"I .... , because ...."

Self-Check

COMMUNICATION CHALLENGE

Pair Work Student A: Look at Challenge 8A on page 119. Student B: Look at Challenge 8B on page 121.

1 Write down five new words you learned in this unit.

....

2 Write sentences using three of these new words.

....

....

....

3 Write down three new sentences or questions you learned.

....

....

....

4 Review the language skills you practiced in this unit. Check [√] your answers.

CAN YOU:

Talk about personal qualities? ☐ yes ☐ a little ☐ not yet

Find or give an example: ....

Give reasons? ☐ yes ☐ a little ☐ not yet

Find or give an example: ....

5 Group Work Discussion. Complete this statement and discuss it.

"*Summarizing* can help develop language skills because

...."

6 Vocabulary check. Check [√] the words you know.

Adjectives/Adverbs			Conjunctions	Nouns			Verbs	
☐ aggressive	☐ gentle	☐ static	☐ because	☐ aggressiveness	☐ diplomat	☐ present	☐ admit	☐ pin
☐ ambitious	☐ loyal	☐ traditional	☐ so	☐ anger	☐ event	☐ quality	☐ fear	☐ rate
☐ angry	☐ married	☐ very		☐ bride	☐ festival	☐ relatives	☐ forget	☐ share
☐ fair	☐ personal	☐ well-educated		☐ career	☐ hatred	☐ selfishness	☐ marry	☐ summarize
☐ jealous	☐ really	☐ witty		☐ ceremony	☐ husband	☐ view		
☐ kind	☐ selfish			☐ competitiveness	☐ kindness	☐ wedding		
☐ kind of	☐ sort of			☐ consensus	☐ loyalty	☐ wife		

9 Older & Younger Folks

Warm-Up

Picture 1

Picture 2

Picture 3

Picture 4

Picture 5

Unit Goals

In this unit you will:

Give opinions

"I think young people need to respect older people."

Evaluate

"Childhood was the least interesting time of my life."

"I found my twenties to be the most stressful time."

1 a Scan the following statements and underline the words and phrases that indicate different times of life.

.... My favorite time of life was when I was <u>a little boy</u>. I liked the freedom of childhood, but I also liked having someone to take care of me.

.... My teenage years were the best of my life. I loved the excitement of doing things for the first time: dating, driving a car, getting a part-time job. . . .

.... I'm in my seventies and this is the best time of my life. I'm retired, so I have time to relax and enjoy my hobbies. I also finally have the chance to take some classes.

.... The best time of my life was my thirties. We were just starting a family at the time, and I loved having little kids at home.

.... My grandchildren find it hard to believe, but my best years were my late forties and fifties! After our children grew up and moved out, my husband and I had more time to spend just with each other.

b Match these statements with the people in the pictures.

c Discussion. What age was/is your favorite? Why? Which age are you looking forward to most?

2 GroupWork Discussion. Describe things you did when you were a child. What was it like where you grew up? How is it different today?

Task Chain 1 "When I'm 64..."

Task 1

Group Work Discussion. Study this photograph. How much can you say about this person? Where do you think he lives? What do you think his occupation was? Do you think he is happy or sad? Make up a life history.

Task 2

a Group Work Discussion. You are going to hear a young girl, her father, and her grandmother talking about growing old. Before you listen, can you predict which of these statements are made by the grandmother? Which are made by the father? Which are made by the daughter? Give reasons for your choices.

.... I have plenty of time to do the things I want.
.... I want to live to a ripe old age.
.... I don't have to go to work.
.... I want to be happy.
.... I can eat whatever I want to whenever I want.
.... I have lots of friends.
.... I love my television.
.... I've never thought about it much.
.... Life is what happens while you're busy planning other things.
.... I don't want to grow old.
.... I'd hate to be poor.

b 🎧 Listen and mark each statement *G* for grandmother, *F* for father, or *D* for daughter.

c Group Work Discussion. Who has the most positive attitudes toward aging? Are the older people more positive or negative than the younger person? Whose opinions are closest to your own? Which person are you least like?

Task 3

a Complete the following survey. Check [√] your answers.

	Agree	*Disagree*
1 Elderly people should be able to work as long as they choose.	☐	☐
2 Society does not take advantage of the experience that old people have.	☐	☐
3 The elderly do not understand today's young people.	☐	☐
4 Young people do not understand the elderly.	☐	☐
5 Old age begins at 70 or older.	☐	☐

ou're invited... go to the movies! meet me for lunch
what do you do?
why
s my family
when neighborhood

b GroupWork Compare your responses with those of three or four other students.

Task 4

a Compare the following survey responses with your responses to the survey in Task 3.

What Does It Mean to Be Old?

At what age do you consider someone "old"? Do you think society is prejudiced against the elderly? Are you afraid of growing old? Your answers to these questions could well reflect your age. According to a national *Parade* survey, older Americans have fewer fears and fewer negative views of aging, while young people worry about the unknown events that time may bring. 93% say the elderly, if healthy, should be allowed to work as long as they choose. 91% say that society does not take advantage of age and experience. 87% think there is prejudice against the elderly. The youngest respondents (18 to 24) are more likely to feel this way than the oldest (65 to 75). 70% say they feel sorry for the elderly, and 60% think that Americans try to ignore the elderly. People aged 18 to 24 are more likely to express these views than those 65 to 75. 66% say the elderly do not understand today's young people, while 88% think young people do not understand the elderly. 66% say that old age begins at 70 or older. The older the respondents, the older the age they define as "old." Among those over 65, only 8% think of people under 65 as old, while 30% of those under 25 say "old" is anywhere from 40 to 64. Overall, 45% of the respondents—and 64% of those 65 and older—think that life for the elderly has gotten better in the last 20 years.

b PairWork Summarize the article by making a list of the beliefs and attitudes in the article and noting whether the majority (more than 50%) of younger and older respondents agree or disagree with each statement. The first one has been done for you. (If the article does not distinguish between "younger" and "older," it means both groups responded in a similar way.)

BELIEF	YOUNGER	OLDER
The elderly should be allowed to work as long as they choose.	agree	agree

c GroupWork Discussion. Do you think the survey results would be the same in your own country? If not, how do you think they would be different?

d How successful were you in this chain? Circle a phrase and compare your answer with the answers of three or four other students.

hopeless   so-so   OK   good   extremely good   excellent

LEARNING STRATEGY

Self-evaluation – checking how well you did on a learning task.

Language Focus 1 Infinitives

1 a Underline the infinitives in the following text. The first one has been done for you.

When Tony was eighteen he wanted <u>to leave</u> home. However, his parents didn't want to let him go. They said that he was too young. Actually, they didn't like to think that he had grown up. They said that he needed to be at least twenty before he could take care of himself. Tony argued that several of his friends had left home and rented an apartment on the other side of town. They needed to find someone else to move in and help pay the rent. Tony said he had decided to go. His parents said to think of them, but it made no difference to him, and he left home anyway.

b Pair Work Compare your responses.

2 Pair Work Make up statements using the cues and the model.

Example: Tony never visits his grandparents.
[not like / think / about old people]
"He doesn't like to think about old people."

a Silvia's parents were sorry when she left. [she / want / share / apartment / with friends]
b Tony left home at eighteen. [brother / asked / go with him]

c My grandmother doesn't mind growing old. [she / likes / do / things many elderly people do]
d Some young people are very helpful to the elderly. [they / love / work / around / home]
e Many elderly people are independent. [not need / have / other people around all the time]

3 Pair Work Ask and answer these questions.

a Where would you like to live when you are elderly?
b What sort of person do you want to be?
c What kinds of things would you like to do when you're older?

4 Which of these verbs can go in the blank?

mind	love	regret	hate	consider	enjoy
avoid	want	deny	need	prefer	decide

"I .... to lie in bed until lunchtime on the weekends."

ou're invited ... go to the movies! meet me for lunch
what do you do?
why
neighborhood

Task Chain 2 Kid's stuff

Task 1

a Think about your childhood. What was . . .

- your favorite game? ....
- your favorite toy? ....
- your favorite food? ....
- a word that described you best? ....

b Group Work Discussion. Who had the most interesting childhood?

Task 2

a 🎧 Listen. You will hear some people talking about their childhood. Which topics do they discuss? Check [√] your answers.

- ☐ what they wanted to be when they grew up
- ☐ where they lived as children
- ☐ what they were like as children
- ☐ what they thought of school
- ☐ their childhood habits
- ☐ their favorite toys and games
- ☐ their favorite foods

b 🎧 Listen again. What do these people say about their childhood? Fill in the chart.

	QUALITIES	WANTED TO BE	FAVORITE FOOD
Silvia			
David			
Cindy			

c 🎧 Pair Work Compare responses, and then listen again to confirm your responses.

"Well, my earliest memory is when I turned three. I had my usual morning nap, and when I woke up, I had my very first birthday party. All my cousins and friends were there and I got lots of presents, including a bike. Unfortunately I ate too much cake and ice cream, and I got sick. So my birthday party ended the way it began, with me in bed."

turned three
morning sleep
woke up
first birthday party
cousins and friends
lots of presents – bike
ate too much cake/ice cream
sick – went back to bed

Task 3

a What is your earliest memory? Make notes about it.

b Group Work Using your notes, tell your classmates about your earliest memory.

Task 4

a Fill in the first column of the survey chart.

	YOU	STUDENT 1	STUDENT 2
What were you like as a child?			
What did you want to be when you grew up?			
What was your favorite food?			
How did you spend your time?			
What were your favorite toys and games?			

b GroupWork Now interview two other students and complete the chart.

Task 5

a PairWork Skim the letters to the editor of a newspaper (at left and below) and decide how old each letter writer is. Write your answers in the *Age* column below.

b PairWork Look again at each letter and decide whether the letter writer thinks that kids today are better or worse than kids in the past. Check [√] your answers.

Writer	Age	Better	Worse	Can't tell
Disgusted	....	☐	☐	☐
Different Today	....	☐	☐	☐
Rebel With Cause	....	☐	☐	☐

c Summarize the differences that the letter writers see between children today and children in the past.

d GroupWork Discussion. Which statements are true in the place where you live or grew up? Which are not true?

To the Editor:

I am writing to complain about the appalling article that appeared in your newspaper last Saturday. The theme of the article was "our terrible kids," and the authors spent most of the article describing how badly behaved today's kids are, compared with those of older generations. Well, let me just say that I don't believe that kids are any worse today than they were in my day. In my day, there were good and bad children, and the same holds true today. Let me tell you that my grandchildren are far more hard-working, knowledgeable, and considerate of old people than most of the kids I went to school with many years ago. I'm proud of my grandkids, and I'm disgusted with the authors of your article.

Disgusted

Dear Editor,

I read with interest your article on the youth of today. However, there are some things that your authors overlook. Things are different today. Life's much faster than it was 30 years ago, and it's much more dangerous now than it was then. My children can't walk to school alone like I used to do; I have to take them. And once they get to school, they have to work a lot harder than I had to. It's no wonder that they sometimes behave badly. However, I have to tell you that their parents are in turn more badly behaved than their grandparents.

Different Today

Dear Sir/Madam,

I agree with some of the things that your article on kids had to say. Kids do have more ways of amusing themselves, with videos, computer games, and many different kinds of electronic toys, and so I imagine that life is less boring than it was 30 or 40 years ago. For people who like taking risks, life today is more exciting. It's also true that we kids don't have to do a lot of the boring chores that our parents had to do. However, I guess the big question remains—is it better to be a kid today? Well, all I can say to your writers is—try doing what today's kids do, and see what you think!

Rebel With Cause

Language Focus 2 Superlative adjectives

1 a 🎧 **Pair Work** Listen. Then practice the conversation.

> **A:** Did you enjoy your childhood?
> **B:** Yes, I did. It was the most enjoyable time of my life.
> **A:** More enjoyable than being an adult?
> **B:** I think so. Life is more exciting now, but it's also more stressful. How about you?
> **A:** The most stressful time for me was when I was a young teenager. These days, life is less stressful, less exciting, but more enjoyable.

b Pair Work Have the conversation again. Use information that is true for you.

2 How many different ways can you think of to complete the following statements?

> *Example:* Going out alone at night is . . .
> - the most dangerous thing to do in my city
> - the least enjoyable way of spending an evening
> - the easiest way of meeting new people

a Commuting long distances is ....
b Living in a large city is ....
c Life for me is ....
d Childhood for me was ....

3 Pair Work Think of questions for these answers and practice them.

a I suppose living in a big city is pretty exciting.
b Let's see. The most relaxing thing is probably watching movies on the VCR.
c My friend Kim is probably the most unusual person I know.
d Visiting the Amazon rain forests was probably the most adventurous thing.
e The least appealing thing about college is the amount of studying you have to do.

4 Pair Work Ask another student these questions.

a What is the most interesting thing about your life?
b What is the most unusual thing about you?
c What is the funniest thing that's ever happened to you?
d What is the least interesting thing about your life?

Self-Check

COMMUNICATION CHALLENGE

PairWork Student A: Look at Challenge 9A on page 120. Student B: Look at Challenge 9B on page 122.

1 Write down five new words you learned in this unit.

....

2 Write sentences using three of these new words.

....

....

....

3 Write down three new sentences or questions you learned.

....

....

....

4 Review the language skills you practiced in this unit. Check [√] your answers.

CAN YOU:

Give opinions? ☐ yes ☐ a little ☐ not yet

Find or give an example: ....

Evaluate? ☐ yes ☐ a little ☐ not yet

Find or give an example: ·..

5 GroupWork Discussion. Complete this statement and discuss it.

"*Self-evaluation* means ...."

6 Vocabulary check. Check [√] the words you know.

Adjectives/Adverbs

☐ adventurous ☐ favorite ☐ relaxing
☐ around ☐ independent ☐ respected
☐ considerate ☐ less ☐ retired
☐ dangerous ☐ more ☐ stressful
☐ disgusted ☐ most ☐ terrible
☐ earliest ☐ older ☐ weird
☐ elderly ☐ prejudiced ☐ younger

Nouns

☐ anticipation ☐ grandchildren ☐ peace
☐ belief ☐ grandmother ☐ respondent
☐ childhood ☐ influence ☐ silence
☐ chore ☐ majority ☐ solitude
☐ excitement ☐ novelist
☐ folks ☐ old age
☐ freedom ☐ opinions

Verbs

☐ deny ☐ experience ☐ regret
☐ distinguish ☐ grow ☐ respect
☐ don't mind ☐ ignore ☐ take
☐ enjoy ☐ plan ☐ turn
☐ evaluate ☐ prefer

10 Review

Task 1

a 🎧 Listen and match the photographs with the conversations.

b 🎧 Listen again and complete the *talking about* and *what happened* columns.

NAME	TALKING ABOUT	WHAT HAPPENED	WHAT THEY SHOULD HAVE DONE
Marcia			
Stan			
Terri			

c Pair Work Look at the photographs and identify Ken, Tania, and Terri's neighbors.

d Pair Work Now complete the *what they should have done* column.

Task 2

a Group Work Discussion. You are going to hear a conversation among three people talking about *street kids*. What is a street kid?

b 🎧 Pair Work Listen and number the topics in the order you hear them.

.... child ran away
.... one child no good
.... child used to steal money
.... a single-parent family—mother and three children
.... only parents with children understand
.... child given help
.... street kids
.... parents at fault
.... a TV show
.... difficulty of being a parent

c 🎧 Group Work Compare your answers with those of another pair, and then listen again to confirm your responses.

Conversation ....

Conversation ....

Conversation ....

Task 3

a GroupWork Survey. Go around the class and ask these questions. Fill in the blanks.

Question	Name	Answer
1 How did you get spending money when you were a child?	....	....
2 What was the most unusual thing that happened to you as a child?	....	....
3 What was the most important thing you had learned by the time you left school?	....	....
4 Where did your family take vacations when you were young?	....	....
5 What was the scariest thing that happened to you when you were a child?	....	....
6 How much English had you learned by the time you were thirteen?	....	....

b PairWork Compare your answers with those of another student.

c GroupWork Discussion. What was the most interesting or unusual answer?

Task 4

"I had just opened the door when the lights went out and my friends sang *Happy Birthday!*"

a PairWork Think of a way of completing these statements.

1 I had just opened the door when ....
2 I had been .... about four days when I met the most wonderful person.
3 He turned up at the party Saturday night. I hadn't seen .... for years.
4 It was awful; when she got to the .... , he had left.
5 I wasn't interested in the .... , because I had already bought one.

b GroupWork Discussion. Which pair has the most creative, unusual, or interesting statements?

Task 5

PairWork Have a conversation using these functions.

A: Think of something you want to borrow from B—for example, a book, some money, or a jacket. Make a polite request.
B: Say no to the request, and give a reason.
A: Accept your partner's reason.

11 The Electronic Age

Warm-Up

Unit Goals

In this unit you will:

Give and follow instructions

"You fill the machine with water, put coffee in here, and turn it on."

Make inquiries

"Can you tell me how much it costs?"

LEARNING STRATEGY

Lateral thinking = thinking of unusual solutions to puzzles or problems.

"Well, working as a radiologist would be difficult to do from home. But if someone invented very high quality, color faxes, hospitals could fax X rays to doctors' homes, and the doctors could use these for diagnosis."

1 a Look at the picture. Make a list of the electronic devices you see.

b Group Work Brainstorm. What other electronic devices can you think of? Add to the list.

2 The woman in the picture is *telecommuting*, or working at home. What do you think are some of the advantages and disadvantages of telecommuting? Would you like to telecommute? Why or why not?

3 Group Work Discussion. What electronic devices make it possible for office workers to telecommute?

4 a Group Work Make a list of occupations that would be easy to do from home and a list of occupations that would be difficult to do from home.

b Group Work Review the occupations that would be difficult to do from home. Can you think of electronic devices that might make it possible to do these jobs from home?

Turn on the VCR

"Have you ever owned a CD player?"

Task 1

a Have you ever used or owned these things? Check [√] your answers in the first two columns.

	You used	You owned	Your Partner used	Your Partner owned	Adjective
1 coffee maker	☐	☐	☐	☐	....
2 toaster	☐	☐	☐	☐	....
3 microwave oven	☐	☐	☐	☐	....
4 fax machine	☐	☐	☐	☐	....
5 CD player	☐	☐	☐	☐	....
6 video player	☐	☐	☐	☐	....
7 personal computer	☐	☐	☐	☐	....
8 personal cassette player	☐	☐	☐	☐	....
9 answering machine	☐	☐	☐	☐	....

Picture 1

Picture 2   Picture 3

Picture 4   Picture 5

Picture 6   Picture 7

Picture 8   Picture 9

b **Pair Work** Now ask another student and check [√] the third and fourth columns.

c **Group Work** Class survey. What are the three most popular devices? What are the three least popular?

d **Pair Work** Find words to describe each device, and complete the last column.

Examples: essential, extravagant, boring, useful, useless, interesting

e **Group Work** Compare your words with another pair's words.

Task 2

a 🎧 Listen to four people talking about how to use different appliances. Which conversations contain these words? Check [√] in the correct column.

	Conversation 1	2	3	4			Conversation 1	2	3	4
1 turn on	☐	☐	☐	☐	6 take out	☐	☐	☐	☐
2 press	☐	☐	☐	☐	7 grind up	☐	☐	☐	☐
3 put on	☐	☐	☐	☐	8 fill up	☐	☐	☐	☐
4 turn over	☐	☐	☐	☐	9 plug in	☐	☐	☐	☐
5 put in	☐	☐	☐	☐	10 turns off	☐	☐	☐	☐

b 🎧 **Pair Work** Listen again and look at these photographs. Which appliances are the people talking about?

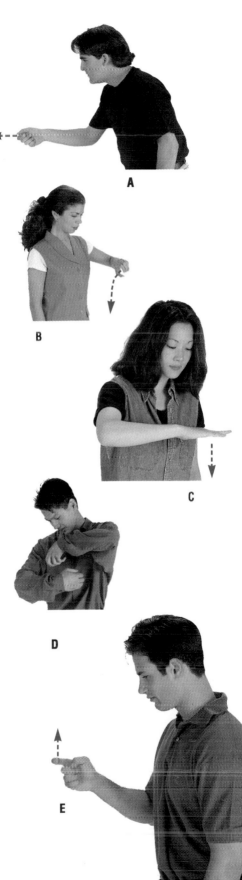

Task 3

a **Pair Work** Can you guess what these people are doing?

b **Pair Work** The teacher will mime some actions. Can you guess them?

c **Group Work** Take turns miming and guessing the verbs.

Task 4

Group Work Discussion. These words are from advertisements for electrical products. What products are they advertising?

a video controller   3.5 and 5.25 floppy drives   modem   mouse monitor sold separately

b stereo color monitor   receiver with remote control advanced picture tube with deep-black screen

c save $3   morning maker   12-cup capacity   pause 'n' serve

Task 5

a **Pair Work** The following text contains instructions for two different electrical appliances. Can you unscramble the instructions? Write *A* or *B* to show which sentence belongs to which set of instructions.

.... Read all instructions carefully.
.... Make sure any ink is dry before feeding it into the machine.
.... Plug the cord into an electrical outlet.
.... Open the door and place the glass tray and roller rings inside.
.... Place the document in the tray face down.
.... Place food at room temperature on the glass tray.
.... Press the MONITOR button to turn on the screen.
.... Close the door.
.... Select power by touching the POWER button.
.... Press the START button.
.... Call up the required number.
.... Set timer according to timer chart.
.... Check that the document feeds through evenly.
.... When timer rings, remove food from cavity.
.... At the completion of the operation, check that the document has been sent successfully.

b What machines do you think the instructions are for?

Task 6

a **Pair Work** Write instructions for an appliance, but don't say what it is.

b **Group Work** Exchange papers with another pair and guess the appliance.

Language Focus 1 Two-part verbs

1 **PairWork** Match the questions and answers and practice them.

.... Why won't the TV work?
.... What's wrong with the coffee machine?
.... Where's the fax message that just came in?
.... How do you use this answering machine?
.... Where's the new computer?

a You need to fill it up with water.
b Push that button down, and you'll hear the messages.
c I asked the secretary to lock it up somewhere safe.
d You didn't turn it on.
e I put it on your desk.

2 🎧 **PairWork** Listen. Then practice the conversation.

A: How do you work this video machine?
B: Well, you plug it in. Then you make sure it's connected to the TV. Then you put in a cassette, sit back, and relax.
A: Hey, why won't it work?
B: You forgot to turn it on.

3 a Check [√] the statements that are correct.

☐ Put in the paper, right here.
☐ Turn on it, at the back here.
☐ When you've finished, turn off it.
☐ Grind up the coffee beans like this.
☐ To stop it, you press it down here.

b Now correct the incorrect statements.

Do you know the rule?

Complete the statements using the words *pronoun* (I, you, he, she, we, they, it) or *noun* (the name of a thing or person).

A .... can go after the two-part verb or between the first part and the second part of the verb.

A .... can only go between the first part and the second part of the verb.

4 a Match the verbs with the prepositions. Each verb can go with more than one preposition.

turn	in
put	on
bring	under
stick	out
fill	over
keep	up

b **PairWork** You are getting ready for a party. Take turns giving instructions using two-part verbs.

Examples: "Could you turn on the popcorn popper?"
"Don't forget to bring out the food."

go to the movies!   meet me for lunch
you're invited . . . .   what do you do?   why
is   why   borhood

Task Chain 2
Can you tell me how much it costs?

And it is easy to program.

Task 1
Where is this person? What does he want to buy?

Task 2
a Group Work You want to buy a new VCR. Make a list of the questions you would like the salesperson to answer.

b Group Work Now compare your list with another group's list.

Task 3
a Listen to a telephone conversation between a customer and a salesperson and complete the chart.

A Can you tell me how much the Inko costs?

B Sure. It costs $895.

MODEL	COST	ADVANTAGES	DISADVANTAGES
Dobson			
Sonic			
Inko			
Nova			

b Pair Work Use the information in the chart to ask and answer questions about the different models.

Task 4

GroupWork Discussion. Which model would be the best for each of these people?

a Your cousin. She is getting a college degree in media studies, and therefore she needs to record numerous programs so she can play them back more than once. Unfortunately, because she is a student, she does not have a lot of money.

b Your brother. He has plenty of money, but he doesn't watch much television or many movies.

c Your sister. She is a journalist and needs to keep informed of events at home and abroad. She wants a VCR so that she can record current affairs programs, many of which are shown at the same time or when she is out.

d Your best friend. He or she is a movie fan and watches lots of movies, both on television and video.

e Your elderly uncle. He has never owned a VCR and is nervous about learning how to use new appliances.

Task 5

You choose: Do **A** or **B**.

A PairWork Pretend to be one of the people in Task 4. Ask your partner for advice about which model to buy. Then change roles and practice again.

B PairWork Discuss the different models above. Which one would be the best for your needs?

Language Focus 2 Indirect questions

1 a Number these sentences in order to make a conversation. There may be more than one correct order.

.... Do you think it has any disadvantages?
.... Let's see. That one's $620.
.... Can you tell me how much the video player costs?
         Well, it has a magic wand.
.... Well, it's last year's model.
.... And can you tell me what special features it has?

b Pair Work Now practice the conversation with another student.

2 a Make indirect questions from the direct questions.

Direct Questions	Indirect Questions
1 How much does it cost?	*Can you tell me how much it costs?*
2 What does it cost?	....
3 What does the wand do?	....
4 Where did you buy the VCR?	....
5 Where do you turn it on?	....
6 When do you watch it?	....

b Pair Work Now make up answers to the questions above and practice them.

3 Pair Work Make indirect questions for these answers and then practice them.

a The Sonic is our least expensive model.
b It costs $480.
c It doesn't have an automatic rewind system.
d A magic wand allows you to program the machine automatically.
e The Nova is our most expensive model.

"Could you tell me if you have a VCR?"

4 a Write several indirect questions you would like to ask students in your class.

b Group Work Take turns asking and answering your questions.

Self-Check

COMMUNICATION CHALLENGE

GroupWork Student A: Look at Challenge 11A on page 113. Student B: Look at Challenge 11B on page 124. Student C: Look at Challenge 11C on page 128.

1 Write down five new words you learned in this unit.

....

2 Write sentences using three of these new words.

....

....

....

3 Write down three new sentences or questions you learned.

....

....

....

4 Review the language skills you practiced in this unit. Check [√] your answers.

CAN YOU:

Give and follow instructions?   ☐ yes   ☐ a little   ☐ not yet
Find or give an example: ....

Make inquiries?   ☐ yes   ☐ a little   ☐ not yet
Find or give an example: ....

5 GroupWork Discussion. How can *lateral thinking* help you learn another language?

6 Vocabulary check. Check [√] the words you know.

Adjectives/Adverbs

☐ appropriate	☐ extravagant	☐ portable
☐ automatically	☐ face-to-face	☐ special
☐ crucial	☐ indirect	☐ successfully
☐ electronic	☐ long-	☐ technological
☐ essential	playing	
☐ evenly	☐ nervous	

Nouns

☐ appliance	☐ fax machine	☐ overwork
☐ capability	☐ feature	☐ program
☐ cassette	☐ inquiries	☐ screen
☐ CD player	☐ instructions	☐ timer
☐ coffee	☐ isolation	☐ toaster
maker	☐ microwave	☐ VCR
☐ completion	oven	☐ warranty
☐ device	☐ model	
☐ document	☐ monitor	

Verbs

☐ commute	☐ mime	☐ quit
☐ convince	☐ offer	☐ take out
☐ cost	☐ own	☐ telecommute
☐ fill up	☐ plug in	☐ turn off
☐ grind up	☐ put in	☐ turn on
☐ manage	☐ put on	☐ turn over

12 Getting Around

Warm-Up

Unit Goals

In this unit you will:

Make comparisons

"Which do you prefer, the bus or the subway?"

"I guess I like the subway better."

Make plans

"I'm going to fly to Spain for my vacation."

Picture 1   Picture 2   Picture 3

Picture 4   Picture 5   Picture 6   Picture 7

1 a Check [√] the words you know. Look up the others in your dictionary.

☐ train	☐ rickshaw	☐ foot	☐ in-line skates	☐ canoe
☐ yacht	☐ subway	☐ bus	☐ hot-air balloon	☐ airplane
☐ ferry	☐ helicopter	☐ car	☐ motorcycle	☐ bicycle

b Which of these things can you find in the photographs above?

2 a Pair Work Classify the above types of transportation. Write the words in the correct columns in the chart.

ON LAND	ON WATER	IN THE AIR

b Group Work Discussion. Which of the types of transportation in the list in 1a have you used? (Circle them.) Which would you like to use? Which methods would you use to go to work? On vacation in your own country? On vacation in another country?

Task Chain 1 Getting to work

Task 1

a What is important to you when choosing transportation to work or school? Rank these factors from least to most important.

.... The service is cheap.
.... The transportation leaves frequently.
.... It is safe.
.... It gets me to work or school quickly.
.... It is comfortable, and I can get a seat.
.... It is convenient.

b GroupWork Compare your results. Which is the most important factor in your group? Which is the least important factor?

c GroupWork Make a list of all the forms of transportation where you live. Then talk about their advantages and disadvantages.

"Well, walking gives me some exercise, but it doesn't get me to work quickly. The train is comfortable, but it costs more."

Task 2

a Listen. You will hear several people talking about how they get to work. How many different forms of transportation do you hear?

b Listen again and match the people and the methods of getting to work.

Helen	walk, bus, subway, walk
Mary	shuttle, subway, walk
Joe	walk, commuter bus, walk

c Listen again and complete the chart. The first one has been done for you.

PERSON	COMMENTS ABOUT BUS	COMMENTS ABOUT TRAIN	PREFERS
Helen	as crowded as train takes longer	quicker than bus	train
Joe			
Mary			

d GroupWork Discussion. How do you get to work or school? Is it a good method of transportation? Why or why not?

Task 3

LEARNING STRATEGY

Top-down reading = using what you already know to understand new written information.

a Read about transportation in Hong Kong and underline the different forms of transportation. How many did you find? Try to use what you know about public transportation to make sense of the text.

There is just one railway system, the Kowloon-Canton Railway, which goes from Kowloon Station in Hung Hom up to the border of China at Lo Wu. From there you can change trains and travel all the way through China, the former Soviet Union, and on to Europe. The 12 green and white ferries have been plying between Central and Tsim Sha Tsui since 1898, and 95 years later one single journey still costs only HK$1.50. The 89-year-old Hong Kong Island electric tram system is known as the "pollution solution." Hong Kong's buses are run by China Motor Bus and Citybus on Hong Kong Island and by Kowloon Motor Bus in Kowloon. For the locals, minibuses are a cheap and practical way of getting around town, but they can be a challenge for the visitor. Maxicabs are the green and yellow versions of minibuses and run on a scheduled route. "Heliservices" operate helicopter charter flights. Clients must charter the whole aircraft for at least 30 minutes. Rickshaws are now seen only around the Star Ferry at Central. They will take you around the block, but make sure you negotiate the price first.

b Summarize the text above by completing the following chart.

FORM OF TRANSPORTATION	CHARACTERISTICS

Task 4

Imagine you are writing a visitor's guide to transportation where you live. Using the text in Task 3 as a model, write about the different forms of transportation.

Language Focus 1 Comparison of adverbs and adjectives

1 a 🎧 Pair Work Listen. Then practice the conversation.

> **A:** Which do you prefer, the bus or the subway?
> **B:** I prefer the subway.
> **A:** Really? Why?
> **B:** Well, the service is more frequent on my bus, but the subway goes farther and faster.

b Pair Work Practice the conversation again. This time use information that is true for you. Try to use some of the adverbs from Task Chain 1.

2 Pair Work Complete the chart, and then make statements using both forms of the word.

Example: "The subway is quick. The bus also goes quickly."

ADJECTIVES	ADVERBS
quick	*quickly*
bad	
	comfortably
	fantastically
	seriously
	terribly
easy	

Do you know the rule?

Complete these statements.

Form most adverbs by adding .... to the adjective.

If the adjective ends in *le,* change the *e* to ....

If the adjective ends in .... , add *ally.*

If the adjective ends in *y,* change the *y* to .... and add ....

3 Fill in the blanks with appropriate adverbs and adjectives.

Public transportation in Bangkok has gone through some remarkable changes over the years. Mainly it has gotten .... and .... In the old days, it used to be .... You could travel to and from the office in a boat, riding .... along a *klong* (stream) in a boat. Until recently, rickshaws were common and provided a .... way of getting around. These days the streets are too .... to ride in a rickshaw. However, taxis and buses are .... and air-conditioned coaches are .... There is one .... thing about Bangkok traffic these days, however. It gives the locals an .... topic of conversation— how .... the traffic is!

4 Find the incorrect sentences and correct them.

a Public transportation in our cities is very well.
b The bus service in our town is getting worse and worse.
c Our trains are very quickly.
d I generally take the subway because it's cheap.
e Mary had an accident and was injured quite serious.

ou're invited ... go to the movies! meet me for lunch
what do you do? why
s neighborhood when

Task Chain 2 We're going to fly to Seoul

Task 1

a Write down the five places in the world you would most like to visit.

....

b What were the reasons for your choices? Make a list.

Examples: lots of nightlife and entertainment; good shopping; spectacular natural scenery; interesting restaurants; different, strange, and interesting customs

c GroupWork Now work with three other students and make a single list of five places.

Task 2

a 🎧 Listen to the first part of the conversation and check the places you hear.

☐ Manila ☐ San Francisco ☐ Singapore ☐ Bangkok
☐ Taiwan ☐ Los Angeles ☐ Hong Kong ☐ Taipei
☐ Seoul ☐ South Korea

b 🎧 Listen again and write out Dan's itinerary.

Day	Date	Place	Reason

Task 3

a 🎧 These are the notes Dan makes about his flight options. Unfortunately, he makes four mistakes. Listen to the second part of the conversation and correct the mistakes.

Asia Airline	$1,900	L.A. – Seoul	Wed.	
		Seoul - Taipei	Every day	
		Taipei - Singapore	Wed.	* via Manila – would miss first part of trade fair
		Singapore - L.A.	Fri.	* would miss last day of trade fair
Southeast	$3,500	L.A. - Seoul	Wed.	* upgrade to business class
		Seoul - Taipei	Mon., Thurs., Fri.	* would miss first day of meeting
		Taipei - Singapore	Wed.	
		Singapore - L.A.	Sun., Tues., Thurs.	* via Tokyo – would miss most of wedding anniversary

b Group Work Discussion. Decide which airline has the best deal for Dan.

Task 4

a Think of some places you would like to visit and write your own itinerary.

Day	Date	Place	Reason
....	....	....	....
....	....	....	....
....	....	....	....
....	....	....	....
....	....	....	....

"Well, on Monday, July 15th, I'm flying to Mexico City for a meeting with my boss."

b Pair Work Take turns describing your itinerary to another student.

c Write a letter to a friend or your family describing the trip you are about to take.

May 14

Dear Monica,
I'm leaving for South America tomorrow.
First I'm going to fly to Venezuela to visit
my cousin in Caracas. Then I'm going to....

Language Focus 2 Future: present progressive, *going to*

1 🎧 **Pair Work** Listen. Then practice the conversation with another student. If possible, use your own information.

A: What are you doing this vacation?
B: I'm going away.
A: Oh, really? Where?
B: Well, first I'm going to fly to Paris for some shopping. Then I'm going to drive to Spain to go skiing. How about you?
A: I'm going to do volunteer work in a vacation camp for homeless kids.

2 a Fill out this planner with your plan for next week. Leave two or three days blank.

Monday: ....
Tuesday: ....
Wednesday: ....
Thursday: ....
Friday: ....
Saturday: ....
Sunday: ....

b **Group Work** Discussion. Now talk about your plans with three other students. Who is going to have the most interesting week?

A What about Monday afternoon?

B That's OK for me—I'm only studying.

C I can't. I'm going shopping with my sister.

A What are you doing Tuesday morning?

C Tuesday morning's fine with me. I'm not doing anything.

3 **Group Work** Work with three other students. You and your classmates need to meet next week to work on a class assignment. Using your daily planner, try to find a time when you can all meet.

4 a **Group Work** Think of something you are going to do in the future. Mime the action, and get the other students in the group to ask questions and guess what you're going to do.

Examples: "Are you going to use an automatic teller machine?"
"Are you going to write your assignment for Thursday?"

b **Group Work** Choose the most interesting or unusual action and share it with the rest of the class.

Self-Check

COMMUNICATION CHALLENGE

Pair Work Look at Challenge 12 on page 123.

1 Write down five new words you learned in this unit.

....

2 Write sentences using three of these new words.

....

....

....

3 Write down three new sentences or questions you learned.

....

....

....

4 Review the language skills you practiced in this unit. Check [√] your answers.

CAN YOU:

Make comparisons?   □ yes   □ a little   □ not yet
Find or give an example: ....

Make plans?   □ yes   □ a little   □ not yet
Find or give an example: ....

5 Group Work Discussion. Complete the following statement.

"In this unit, using *top-down reading* strategies helped me to understand the transportation text on Hong Kong because ...."

6 Vocabulary check. Check [√] the words you know.

Adjectives/Adverbs

□ banned	□ easy	□ natural	□ special
□ business	□ fantastically	□ quick	□ spectacular
□ comfortable	□ farther	□ quickly	□ terribly
□ comfortably	□ fewer	□ serious	□ valid
□ crowded	□ forbidden	□ seriously	□ worse

Nouns

□ anniversary	□ in-line	□ subway
□ date line	skates	□ trade fair
□ deal	□ itinerary	□ traffic jam
□ ferry	□ nightlife	□ transportation
□ flight	□ options	□ vacation
□ helicopter	□ questionnaire	□ yacht
□ hot-air	□ rickshaw	
balloon	□ shuttle bus	

Verbs

□ charter	□ miss
□ create	□ upgrade
□ fly	

13 Slaves to Fashion

Warm-Up

Unit Goals

In this unit you will:

Express preferences

"Would you rather be fashionable or comfortable?"

"I prefer being comfortable."

Make complaints

"I was overcharged."

"I like casual clothes because I'd rather be comfortable than fashionable. I wear a lot of denim, because it's casual but also stylish."

1 Look at the picture. Which fashions do you like? Why?

2 a Listen. What does the person say about grunge? Make a list of the kind of things a person who likes grunge fashion might wear. Does anybody in the picture follow this fashion?

   b Has this fashion ever been popular in your country?

3 a What does *trendy* mean? Read this conversation and underline the words that help you understand the meaning.

    A: Andre looks trendy today.
    B: Yes, he's always wearing the latest fashions.

   b Do you know any trendy looking people? What kinds of clothes do they wear?

Task Chain 1 I'd rather wear jeans

Task 1

a Group Work Brainstorm. How many different ways can you think of to group clothing words?

Examples: men's and women's, formal and informal, summer and winter

b Group Work Brainstorm. How many clothing words can you think of?

Examples: shoes, jacket, hat, shirt, sweatshirt, ski pants, tie, jogging shorts, jeans, T-shirt

c Group Work Exchange lists with another group, and put their words together in groups that make sense to you.

Task 2

a 🎧 Listen to the conversation about fashion. Who wears these things? Write the appropriate letter in each blank—*A* for Andre, *N* for Nancy, and *S* for Sarah.

.... denim shirt	.... collarless shirt	.... vest
.... leather boots	.... leather jacket	.... suspenders
.... denim skirt	.... leather skirt	

b 🎧 Listen again. Who cares about fashion and who doesn't? What do they look for when buying clothes?

Name	Yes	No	Not sure	Reason for buying clothing
Sarah	☐	☐	☐	....
Andre	☐	☐	☐	....
Nancy	☐	☐	☐	....

c Look at the picture at the beginning of the unit and find Nancy, Sarah, and Andre.

Task 3

a Group Work Brainstorm and make a list of the current fashions under the following headings.

CLOTHING	MUSIC	MOVIES
platform shoes	rap	horror

"I think that the fashion for platform shoes won't last long. They're too uncomfortable and dangerous for people to take them seriously."

b GroupWork Compare your list with another group's list and note similarities and differences.

c GroupWork Discussion. Predict how long these fashions will last.

Task 4

a In this task, you are going to read an article called "The Psychology of Sales." What do you think it is about?

b Here are some of the key words and phrases in the article. What do you think are the main points in the article?

sales . . . competitive . . .
beat the system . . . something for nothing . . .
aggressive way to shop . . . women's growing sense of power . . .
control in society . . . refusing to spend . . . lower their prices . . .
a deal . . . power of suggestion . . . our fall sale . . .

c Now read the article and confirm your predictions.

Why sales work: they make us competitive and make us want to beat the system and get something for nothing. "They're an aggressive way to shop. There are elbows flying and you have to hunt a little," says Manhattan psychotherapist Linda Barbanell. "Sales relate to women's growing sense of power," says New York City psychologist Judy Gold, Ph.D. "As women have gained more control in society, they have gained power over storeowners by refusing to spend large amounts of money, forcing the owners to lower their prices." Of course, the storeowners can use these competitive urges to their own ends. "People don't want to miss out on a deal, so the power of suggestion is incredible," says J. C. Penney executive vice

president Gale Duff-Bloom. "During our fall sale, shoppers used to buy single items—a shirt here, a jacket there. When we changed the name to wardrobe sale, people began buying suits, shirts, shoes, and all the supporting pieces."

Others argue that sales are a form of confidence trick, that goods aren't that much cheaper at all. "It's all an illusion," says consumer advocate Ralph Williams. "People get home from the excitement of the sale to find they've spent heaps of money on things they didn't really need and will probably never wear. My advice is—if you really need it and can afford it, go buy it. Don't worry about whether it's on sale or not."

d GroupWork Discussion. Do you go to sales? Talk about the last sale you went to. Did you get any bargains? What were they? Do you think you really get bargains at sales?

Task 5

GroupWork Discussion. What are the fashion trends in your country now?

Language Focus 1 *Would rather, prefer*

1 🎧 **PairWork** Listen, and then practice the conversation.

A: Would you rather wear fashionable or comfortable clothes?
B: Oh, I prefer being fashionable.
A: Really?
B: Sure.
A: Then why are you wearing that flannel vest and those baggy jeans?
B: Oh, this is grunge. It's the latest fashion.
A: Well, if that's fashionable, I'd rather be unfashionable!

2 a Which of these are true for you?

1 "Oh, I much prefer being comfortable."
2 "I would rather wear fashionable things than unfashionable things if I have the choice."
3 "I prefer to wear jeans and a T-shirt whenever possible."
4 "I would rather buy stuff that's cheap and comfortable than stuff that's trendy."
5 "Well, I'd prefer being comfortable and fashionable."

b **PairWork** Compare your choices with another student's choices.

3 a Make questions using *Would you rather . . . ?* and *Do you prefer . . . ?*

1 .... wearing fashionable or comfortable clothing?
2 .... shop in a boutique or a department store?
3 .... buying jeans or suits?
4 .... spending money on clothing or entertainment?
5 .... read fashion magazines or sports magazines?
6 .... ?
7 .... ?
8 .... ?

b **PairWork** Add three more questions to the list above.

4 **GroupWork** Use the questions in 3a to interview three other students.

you're invited... go to the movies! meet me for lunch
what do you do? why
s neighborhood when

Task Chain 2 I was overcharged

Task 1

GroupWork Brainstorm. Make a list of the things that group members have bought that they haven't been happy with.

ITEM	COMPLAINT	ACTION
watch	battery died within a week	returned it to the store for a replacement battery

Task 2

a 🎧 Listen and complete the chart.

WHERE EVENT TOOK PLACE	WHAT WAS BOUGHT	COMPLAINT	RESULT

b 🎧 PairWork Listen again and check your responses with another student.

"I asked for a table by the window, but I was given a table at the back of the restaurant."

Task 3

GroupWork What would you say? Take turns making a complaint in the following places.

a In a hotel. You asked for a room with a view, but you have been given a room facing a brick wall.

b In a restaurant. You are in the nonsmoking section, and someone lights a cigarette.

c In a store. You bought a pair of shoes, but one of the heels came off after a week.

Task 4

PairWork What kinds of things might you complain about in these places? Make a list and practice making the complaints.

a in a hotel   c on public transportation
b at school   d in an electronics store

Task 5

You choose: Do **A** or **B**.

A **Pair Work** Compare the store policies at left and answer the questions by writing *yes* or *no* in the chart.

	BLOOMFIELD'S	SMITH'S	P.C. LEE
Evidence of purchase required?			
Only if faulty?			
Only up to one month from purchase?			

Bloomfield's will accept merchandise for exchange only up to one calendar month from the date of purchase. Merchandise must be returned to the exchange department in the store where you made the purchase.

Smith's accepts merchandise for exchange only if it is accompanied by the original receipt. Merchandise can be exchanged up to four weeks from the time of purchase.

P. C. Lee Ltd. *accepts merchandise for exchange only if it is faulty. Merchandise to be exchanged must be accompanied by a receipt or other proof of purchase.*

B Read the following letter of complaint. What kind of company is the person writing to? Underline the complaints.

December 17

Attn.: Julie or Shannon, Customer Service
Fax: 555-3972
RetroVision
P.O. Box 30403
Las Vegas NV 89132
Re: Account # 93857

For the third consecutive month my bill has been incorrect. I believe that I owe $24.02 for basic service with a box and nothing more. I've never ordered the special movie service, and I've never ordered a premium channel, except for the $1.99 limited-time specials. I've also paid all my bills the minute I've received them. (However, the October bill was never sent; I had to call to get the amount!)

Last month Julie said she would fix this mess, but the billing is still wrong. Furthermore, I have an undeserved late charge. Why do I have to call every month?

Please let me know the outcome by fax or phone, and PLEASE update my account. Thank you!

Sincerely,
Eileen Anderson

Group Work Discussion. What would you do if you were Eileen?

Task 6

Group Work Discussion. In your country, what is the attitude toward returning something to a store? How do you return something? Is there usually a time limit on when you can return things? Can you get a cash refund, or do stores generally only make exchanges?

Language Focus 2 Passive voice

1 🎧 **Pair Work** Listen, and then practice the conversation.

A: I had a terrible day.

B: Really? What happened?

A: I decided to go to that new restaurant for lunch.

B: And you didn't like it?

A: No. I had a reservation, but I was kept waiting for half an hour. Then I was put in the smoking section. After the meal, I was overcharged, and when I complained, I was insulted.

B: Sounds like a good place to avoid.

2 a **Group Work** Where do you think you would hear these complaints? Think of as many situations as you can for each one.

1 I was kept waiting for ages.   *in a department store, at the airport, in a restaurant*

2 We were shouted at.   ....

3 I was overcharged.   ....

4 He was rewarded.   ....

5 I wasn't invited.   ....

b **Group Work** Compare responses. Which group has the most unusual, the most interesting, and the most unlikely responses?

3 **Pair Work** Make up statements following the model.

Active	*Passive*
a Someone overcharged me.	*I was overcharged.*
b Someone stole my shopping bag.	....
c Someone left Paul a nice gift.	....
d No one served me.	....
e They closed the store early.	....

4 Turn these newspaper headlines into complete sentences using passive statements.

a Record Price Paid for Abstract Painting
   A record price was paid for an abstract painting.

b Diamond Necklace Stolen From Tiffany's

....

c *Million Dollar Necklace Uninsured*

....

d Thief Caught at Airport

....

Self-Check

COMMUNICATION CHALLENGE

PairWork Student A: Look at Challenge 13A on page 125. Student B: Look at Challenge 13B on page 128.

1 Write down five new words you learned in this unit.

....

2 Write sentences using three of these new words.

....

....

....

3 Write down three new sentences or questions you learned.

....

....

....

4 Review the language skills you practiced in this unit. Check [√] your answers.

CAN YOU:

Express preferences? □ yes □ a little □ not yet

Find or give an example: ....

Make complaints? □ yes □ a little □ not yet

Find or give an example: ....

5 **GroupWork** Discussion. How useful do you find *grouping* as a way of learning new words?

6 Vocabulary check. Check [√] the words you know.

Adjectives/Adverbs

□ baggy	□ fashionable	□ informal
□ competitive	□ faulty	□ latest
□ consecutive	□ flannel	□ popular
□ cool	□ formal	□ stylish
□ current	□ incredible	□ trendy

Nouns

□ bill	□ follower	□ reason
□ boutique	□ grunge	□ reservation
□ complaint	□ illusion	□ sales
□ confidence trick	□ outcome	□ suggestion
	□ power	□ suspenders
□ consumer advocate	□ preference	□ trend
	□ psychology	□ vest
□ fashion	□ purchase	

Verbs

□ avoid	□ force	□ return
□ beat	□ group	□ would rather
□ care	□ lower	
□ complain	□ overcharge	
□ exchange	□ refuse	

14 Word Power

Warm-Up

Picture 1

Picture 2

Picture 3

Unit Goals

In this unit you will:

Ask for and give explanations

"How did you learn Portuguese?"

"By living in Brazil for three years."

Describe goods and services

"That's Diane's fabulous red sports car in the parking lot."

LEARNING STRATEGY

Reflecting = thinking about ways you learn best.

Picture 4

1 **Group Work** Look at these pictures from advertisements. What do you think each is trying to sell?

2 a 🎧 Listen. You will hear four people—Maria, Ken, Claudia, and Peter—answering the question "How did you learn another language?" Write the strategies you hear.

Maria ....

Ken ....

Claudia ....

Peter ....

b **Group Work** Discussion. Imagine that these four people are joining the class. Which student would you most like to work with? Which student would you least like to work with? Discuss your choices with three other students, and give reasons.

Task Chain 1 How did you learn Portuguese?

"I learn to speak by role-playing with friends. I improve my pronunciation by practicing in the language laboratory."

Picture 1

Picture 2

Picture 3

Picture 4

Task 1

a Make a list of the things that help you learn or practice the following skills.

speaking: ....
listening: ....
reading: ....
writing: ....
grammar: ....
vocabulary: ....
pronunciation: ....

b Pair Work Share your list with another student.

Task 2

Pair Work These students are all learning another language. Make a list of the strategies they are using and talk about them.

Task 3

a 🎧 Listen to people talking about how they learned a language and write down the languages you hear them mention.

b 🎧 Listen again. What strategies did the people use to learn languages?

NAME	LANGUAGES	STRATEGIES
1 Byron		
2 Monica		
3 George		

c 🎧 Pair Work Compare answers, and listen again to confirm them.

Task 4

a Group Work Discussion. Do you think that different people learn languages in different ways?

Picture 5

Picture 6

ou're invited... go to the movies! meet me for lunch
what do you do? why
s my family when neighborhood

b Read the following texts. The teachers who wrote them have different opinions about how people learn languages. Note the differences.

TEXT 1

It is a basic fact that learning another language requires hard work and long hours of study. It isn't, and should not be considered, "fun." Being a good learner involves sitting at a desk receiving knowledge from the teacher, taking notes and memorizing them. Before going into class, you should prepare for the lesson by looking up new vocabulary and translating words and texts you don't understand. In class, you should listen carefully to the teacher. And after the lesson is finished, you should review the lesson by memorizing new grammar and vocabulary. If the teacher does not give you materials to prepare before the lesson, you should ask for them. Be wary of teachers who try to get you to interact with each other in class. This is just a form of playing games and is not learning.

TEXT 2

In our school, I have found that language students do not like classes in which they sit passively, reading or translating. Nor do they like classes where the teacher controls everything. It is clear to me that the great majority of English classes are failing to satisfy learner needs in any way. We need major changes in the content of courses and especially in the types of courses that are offered. Most importantly, teachers need to be retrained so that they can get learners actively interacting and communicating with each other in class.

c GroupWork Discussion. Which writer do you agree with most? (There is no "right" answer.) Both teachers work in the same school. Why do you think they have such different opinions?

Task 5

PairWork How do you and your friends like to learn? Make a list of things you like and things you don't like, and discuss them with another student.

This is what one student said.

I like to . . .	*I don't like to . . .*
have conversations with other students	study grammar rules
discuss things with the teacher	do writing tasks
do role-playing and problem-solving tasks	do drills

Language Focus 1 Prepositional phrases with *by*

1 a 🎧 Pair Work Listen. Then practice the conversation.

> **A:** Do you speak any other languages?
> **B:** Yes, I do—Chinese and German.
> **A:** How did you learn them?
> **B:** Well, I learned German by studying it in school, learning the grammar and doing drills.
> **A:** And what about Chinese?
> **B:** Oh, I learned Chinese by living in Taiwan.

b Pair Work Now practice the conversation again. This time, use information that is true for you.

2 Pair Work Match the questions and answers. (There may be more than one possible answer for each question.)

.... How did you learn Portuguese?
.... How did you learn grammar?
.... How do you memorize vocabulary?
.... How can I improve my pronunciation?
.... How did Chen Hong improve her listening?
.... How can I find out about learning Korean?

a By contacting the local consulate or university.
b By watching lots of movies.
c By working in the language laboratory.
d By taping flash cards to the bedroom mirror.
e By memorizing rules.
f By living in Rio de Janeiro.

3 Pair Work Take turns asking and answering these questions. Use the word *by* and the *-ing* form of a verb in each answer.

a How do you learn new vocabulary?
b How do you learn new grammatical structures?
c How do you improve your pronunciation?
d How do you improve your listening skills?
e How do you improve your speaking skills?
f How do you improve your reading skills?
g How do you improve your writing skills?

Task Chain 2 The power of words

Task 1

a Classify these words by writing them in the chart.

wool striped Canadian expensive nice linen green Portuguese Korean fabulous cotton wooden checked Taiwanese cheap black

COLOR/PATTERN	NATIONALITY	QUALITY	MATERIAL

b **Pair Work** Compare your answers with another student's answers.

Task 2

a 🎧 Listen to the radio advertisements and complete the following chart.

NAME OF PRODUCT	TYPE OF PRODUCT	BENEFITS/CLAIMS
1		
2		
3		
4		
5		

b 🎧 **Group Work** Listen to the advertisements again. Which do you like best? Which do you like least? Why? Which does the best job of selling its product?

Task 3

a Read the advertisement at left, and underline the words that give additional information about the nouns in the advertisement. (The first three have been underlined for you.)

b Now make a list of all the claims in the advertisement.

Transit Air Announces <u>New</u>, <u>Simple</u>, <u>Cheaper</u> Fares

Transit Air announces new, simplified prices for flights throughout the world. The result is fantastic values and convenience for customers. Both frequent fliers and once-a-year fliers will get the best deal by flying Transit Air. Transit Air's new full-fare coach price offers you a flexible and convenient ticket. Instant-saver fares offer you up to 40% off the old coach fares.

Task 4

a Match the following products and slogans.

.... credit card   .... airline   .... automobile
.... cologne   .... footwear   .... soft drink

1 It's the real thing.
2 Bumper-to-bumper goose bumps.
3 The look that never wears out.
4 We love to fly and it shows.
5 Live the romance.
6 Don't leave home without it.

"The footwear slogan is trying to suggest that the shoes are high-quality as well as fashionable."

b Group Work Discussion. What are the slogans trying to suggest to the buyer?

c Group Work Discussion. How important do you think it is for advertisers to be honest in promoting their products? Why?

Task 5

a Group Work Develop an advertising campaign for one of the following products. Think of a name, a slogan, and where or how you would advertise the product. Then write the advertisement.

a new drink to rival Coca-Cola
a low-cost, no-frills airline
a nonalcoholic beer
a horror movie
a holiday resort in Tahiti
a cure for baldness

b Group Work Now share your group's advertisement with the class.

Language Focus 2 Word order of modifiers

"I saw two interesting French poodles yesterday."

1 🎧 PairWork Listen. Then practice the conversation.

A: Who owns the fabulous green sports car?
B: I do, as a matter of fact. Why?
A: Oh, I just love cars, especially sports cars.
B: Do you own a car?
A: No, but I have a truck. That's it over there.
B: Where?
A: There. The old red pickup that's half-rusted.

2 a Put the words in each line in the correct order.

1 plastic old red three
2 Japanese a silver modern
3 colorful American two new
4 English secondhand gray
5 French two interesting

b PairWork Now decide what things you could describe using the words above. Take turns making statements.

c GroupWork Discussion. Which pair has the most unusual or humorous statement?

3 Make descriptive statements using the modifiers in Task Chain 2, Task 1.

a _Charlie is wearing a nice, checked, Canadian wool jacket_
b ....
c ....
d ....

4 a PairWork How many modifying words can you add to the spaces provided in this story?

Yesterday I was standing on a .... street. I saw a man and a .... woman drive up in a .... car. The woman, who was wearing a .... dress and carrying a .... bag, got out of the car and went into a .... jewelry store. A short time later she ran out of the store and jumped into the car, and it sped away. A .... man came out of the jewelry store and started shouting. Shortly after that, a .... police car came racing past. I wonder what it was all about.

b PairWork Take turns telling the story.

Do you know the rule?

Study these phrases, and then number the categories to show the order in which modifying words occur. (Examples of categories are shown in parentheses.)

three boring English books

two green metal chairs

an interesting new rock group

fascinating wooden Scandinavian furniture

.... geographical origin
        (Japanese)
.... material (cotton)
.... opinion (silly)
.... color (red)
.... number (five)
.... age (middle-aged)

Self-Check

COMMUNICATION CHALLENGE

PairWork Look at Challenge 14 on page 126.

1 Write down five new words you learned in this unit.

....

2 Write sentences using three of these new words.

....

....

....

3 Write down three new sentences or questions you learned.

....

....

....

4 Review the language skills you practiced in this unit. Check [√] your answers.

CAN YOU:

Ask for and give explanations?   ☐ yes   ☐ a little   ☐ not yet
Find or give an example: ....

Describe goods and services?   ☐ yes   ☐ a little   ☐ not yet
Find or give an example: ....

5 GroupWork Discussion. Complete the following statement.

"*Reflecting* means .... It helps us become better learners because ...."

6 Vocabulary check. Check [√] the words you know.

Adjectives/Adverbs

☐ Canadian	☐ cotton	☐ organized
☐ cheap	☐ expensive	☐ secondhand
☐ checked	☐ fabulous	☐ simplified
☐ clear	☐ frustrated	☐ striped
☐ colorful	☐ humorous	☐ wary
☐ convenient	☐ linen	☐ wool

Nouns

☐ benefit	☐ materials	☐ product
☐ claim	☐ memory	☐ schedule
☐ context	aids	☐ slogan
☐ explanation	☐ parking lot	☐ strategy
☐ formula	☐ pressure	☐ uncertainty

Verbs

☐ appeal	☐ experiment	☐ require
☐ confirm	☐ improve	☐ retrain
☐ contact	☐ interact	☐ tape
☐ establish	☐ memorize	

Mia

Michael

Tomoko

"Tomoko is finding and reading signs and notices in English."

Claudia

Anselm

Task 1

Group Work Discussion. These people are improving their English outside of class. Talk about what they are doing.

Task 2

a **Group Work** Class survey. Go around the class and ask these questions. Fill in the chart.

1 What are you going to do when this English course is finished?
2 Where do you think you'll be this time next year?
3 What are you doing after class?
4 When are you next planning to go to a movie, a concert, or the theater?
5 How much better is your English going to be this time next year?

QUESTION	NAME	ANSWER
1		
2		
3		
4		
5		

b **Group Work** Discussion. What was the most interesting or unusual answer?

Task 3

a 🎧 Listen to the conversation. Which of the following phrases best describes the conversation? Check [√] your answer.

☐ nonverbal communication
☐ ways of communicating with people who don't speak English
☐ coffee-break conversations

b 🎧 Listen again and match the people and their methods of communicating with people who don't speak English.

Frank	uses hands
Tom	draws pictures
Carl	shouts
Nancy	talks slowly
Martha	

c Pair Work Share your answers with another student.

"Carl communicates by speaking slowly."

A Well, you have to put a tape in and put a message on it, and you switch it on when you go out.

B It's an answering machine.

Task 4

Group Work Choose an appliance, but don't say what it is. Make statements about the appliance. The group will guess what it is. Use expressions like these: *plug in, turn on, put in, take out.*

Task 5

Fill in the blanks using words from the following list.

**easy   easily   serious   seriously   terrible   terribly
bad   badly   comfortable   comfortably   quick   quickly**

a Kenji is a .... learner, but Eri learns even more .... than Kenji.

b Graciella said the exam was .... She thinks she will pass ....

c Kim did .... on the exam. Sally turned in a .... exam too.

d Did you study .... when you were learning Japanese? You seemed to be a very .... student.

Task 6

a Pair Work Have a conversation using these cues.

A: Think of a complaint to make and complain to B.
B: Give an explanation to A.
A: Accept or reject B's explanation.

b Pair Work Now change roles and practice the conversation again.

Communication Challenges

Challenge 1

Task 1

Complete the following social survey. Check [√] your answers.

What kind of person are you?			
Are you a person who . . .	Yes	No	Sometimes
a likes to stay out late?	☐	☐	☐
b enjoys learning English?	☐	☐	☐
c is happy in your work?	☐	☐	☐
d loves to have new experiences?	☐	☐	☐
e expects to make a lot of money?	☐	☐	☐
f wants to travel?	☐	☐	☐
g thinks your life is interesting?	☐	☐	☐
h likes excitement?	☐	☐	☐
i enjoys taking risks?	☐	☐	☐
j prefers going out to staying home?	☐	☐	☐

A Are you a person who likes to stay out late?

B Well, sometimes I like to stay out late.

Task 2

Group Work Now walk around the class and find someone who is similar to you. Then find someone who is different from you.

Challenge 2A

Task 1

Pair Work You are making a phone call to your brother or sister. It is his or her birthday. You want him or her to meet you after school in front of the school so that you can give him or her a birthday present.

Task 2

Pair Work You receive a phone call. The person on the other end wants to speak to someone. That person is not in. Ask the person to leave a message. Take the message, and then check that it is correct.

Challenge 4A

"Just imagine. I'm on my first date with Roberto. We're sitting in a restaurant, and Roberto orders a bottle of wine. He is holding my hand, and I'm feeling really romantic. Then this waiter comes out and says that a hurricane is heading for town. Roberto says we have to go. I ask why, and he says that his niece is home alone and she'll be terrified. He insists we go home to see if she's OK, and he heads for the door."

Pair Work At left, Carol is talking about where she and Roberto were and what they were doing when a hurricane hit town. Your partner has Roberto's version of the story. Report what Carol says to your partner and find differences in the two stories. Begin like this: "Carol said that she was on her first date with Roberto. . . ."

Challenge 3A

Pair Work You are asking a famous futurologist what things will be like in the future. Find out about the following topics and take notes. (You can write your own topics in the blank if you wish.)

a work
b transportation
c entertainment
d education
e ....

"What will work be like in the future?"

Challenge 11A

Group Work Work with two other students. You are sharing an apartment with your friends, and you decide to buy a television set. Each of you has a different advertisement. Share your information and decide which set you should buy.

You don't watch a great deal of television, and therefore you like this TV set because it is inexpensive. You definitely do not want to spend more than $400.

$3.23 per week or $349

Neat **51cm Color TV.**
Fashionable black finish.
Audio and video input and output. Portable stand.
5-year warranty.

Challenge 2B

Task 1

PairWork You receive a phone call. The person on the other end wants to speak to someone. That person is not in. Ask the person to leave a message. Take the message, and then check that it is correct.

Task 2

PairWork You are making a phone call to your boyfriend, girlfriend, husband, wife, or best friend at his or her office. You are having a small party this evening and you want him or her to pick up some food and drink on his or her way home.

Challenge 4B

"Well, I'm on my second or third date with Carol. We decide to go out for dinner, and we're sitting in this taxi, heading downtown. Suddenly, a hurricane alert comes over the cab radio. Carol immediately says she has to go home to be with her sister, so home we go. Some date!"

PairWork At left, Roberto is talking about where he and Carol were and what they were doing when a hurricane hit town. Your partner has Carol's version of the story. Listen to your partner and report any differences in the story.

Example: "But Roberto said that they were on their second or third date."

Challenge 3B

PairWork You are a famous futurologist. You are being interviewed about what things will be like in the future. Use these notes to answer the questions.

a *Work:* Most people will be able to work part-time; if there's no work, people will get money from the government.
b *Transportation:* Cars will be banned from cities; you will be able to use high-speed buses and trains.
c *Entertainment:* You will be able to call up movies through your TV.
d *Education:* There won't be any schools; learning programs will be beamed into each home through the TV.

Answers

Here are the answers for the survey in Unit 1, Task Chain 1, Tasks 5 and 6:

Occupation	Rank	Held mostly by . . .
teacher	6	women
airline pilot	2	men
chemical engineer	3	men
lawyer	1	men
pharmacist	4	men
social worker	8	women
architect	5	men
cashier	10	women
cab driver	9	men
plumber	7	men

Challenge 6A

Task 1

Study the following statements. Can you guess who the statements are about? (They may be famous people in history, or they may still be alive.)

Mystery person A: "He used to be a Hollywood movie actor."
I think that this person is ....

Mystery person B: "He used to be Mr. Universe.
He was born in Europe."
I think that this person is ....

Mystery person C: "She used to be married to a famous baseball player and a famous writer. She died young."
I think that this person is ....

Mystery person D: "He used to write pop songs with a famous singer-songwriter who was murdered."
I think that this person is ....

Task 2

a PairWork Now talk to your partner, and decide between you who these people are.

Mystery person A: ....
Mystery person B: ....
Mystery person C: ....
Mystery person D: ....

b PairWork Check your answers on page 119.

Challenge 7

Task 1

Pair Work Complete the following survey. If you haven't been to another country, try to imagine what would bother you. Check [√] your answers.

This bothered me . . .	a lot	a little	not at all
a the weather	☐	☐	☐
b the food	☐	☐	☐
c getting around	☐	☐	☐
d tipping	☐	☐	☐
e language	☐	☐	☐
f social customs	☐	☐	☐
g being away from home	☐	☐	☐
h meeting people	☐	☐	☐
i money matters	☐	☐	☐
j shopping	☐	☐	☐

A Did the weather in England bother you?

B Yes, it did. It rained all the time.

A You should have gone to Spain.

Task 2

Pair Work Find a partner and survey him or her. Check [√] the answers. Give your partner some advice on the things that bothered him or her.

This bothered my partner . . .	a lot	a little	not at all
a the weather	☐	☐	☐
b the food	☐	☐	☐
c getting around	☐	☐	☐
d tipping	☐	☐	☐
e language	☐	☐	☐
f social customs	☐	☐	☐
g being away from home	☐	☐	☐
h meeting people	☐	☐	☐
i money matters	☐	☐	☐
j shopping	☐	☐	☐

"The weather in England bothered Dale a lot. He should have gone to Spain instead."

Task 3

Group Work Tell the class about your partner's answers.

Challenge 6B

Task 1

Study the following statements. Can you guess who the statements are about? (They may be famous people in history, or they may still be alive.)

Mystery person A: "He used to be president of the United States."
I think that this person is ....

Mystery person B: "He used to play a warrior named Conan and a killer robot in the movies."
I think that this person is ....

Mystery person C: "She used to be a famous movie star. Some people say she was murdered."
I think that this person is ....

Mystery person D: "He used to belong to the most popular rock band in the world."
I think that this person is ....

Task 2

a PairWork Now talk to your partner, and decide between you who these people are.

Mystery person A: ....
Mystery person B: ....
Mystery person C: ....
Mystery person D: ....

b PairWork Check your answers on page 119.

ou're invited . . .   go to the movies!   meet me for lunch
what do you do?   why
s my family   when   neighborhood

Challenge 8A

Task 1

Pair Work Here is some information about two women. Your partner has information about two men. Decide which woman would be the best match for which man and give reasons. Use the following model.

"I think that .... and .... would be a good match, because ...."

TESSA

Age:	28
Ambition as a child:	To be a doctor.
Background:	Born in Hungary; came to U.S. at age 6. Went to high school in Washington, D.C. Graduated from Georgetown University with a degree in modern languages.
Occupation:	Interpreter/translator.
Interests:	Dining out, reading, going to parties.
Personal qualities:	Cheerful, honest, easy-going.

VANESSA

Age:	25
Ambition as a child:	To be an Olympic gymnast.
Background:	Born and educated in Brazil. Graduated from university with a major in English.
Occupation:	Teacher and short-story writer.
Interests:	Music of all kinds, dancing, movies, aerobics.
Personal qualities:	Intelligent, full of fun, very friendly; also has a serious side.

Task 2

Group Work Work with another pair. Discuss your choices, and compare the reasons why you made the choices you did.

Answers

Here are the answers to Challenges 6A and 6B:

A = Ronald Reagan	B = Arnold Schwarzenegger
C = Marilyn Monroe	D = Paul McCartney

Challenge 9A

Task 1

PairWork You are interviewing David Glenning, a famous actor, for a magazine article. Find out the following information, and take notes.

- date of birth
- where he grew up
- what he was like as a child
- what he wanted to be
- favorite food
- favorite toy or game
- how he spent his time

Task 2

PairWork You are Sandy Stone, a famous singer. You are being interviewed by a reporter. Use the following information to answer the reporter's questions.

- born in Miami on January 16, 30 years ago
- moved to San Francisco when three years old; grew up there
- as a child: very lively, always playing tricks on people
- wanted to be an architect
- used to eat chili peppers—considered weird for a kid
- can't remember having a favorite toy or game
- spent time making things out of pieces of wood

Challenge 8B

Task 1

Pair Work Here is some information about two men. Your partner has information about two women. Decide which man would be the best match for which woman and give reasons. Use the following model.

"I think that .... and .... would be a good match, because ...."

NICK
Age: 30
Ambition as a child: To be a writer.
Background: Born in Vancouver, Canada. Graduated from University of British Columbia with a degree in French language and literature.
Occupation: Associate professor of French.
Interests: Tennis, classical music, gardening, cooking.
Personal qualities: Quiet, but sometimes has a temper; rather serious but also has a sense of humor; difficult to get to know and hides his true feelings.

BRET
Age: 28
Ambition as a child: To be a musician.
Background: Finished high school, trained as electronics technician, then trained in computing.
Occupation: Computer programmer.
Interests: Jogging, travel, going to parties and dance clubs, rock music.
Personal qualities: Charming, outgoing, social, the life of the party.

Task 2

Group Work Work with another pair. Discuss your choices, and compare the reasons why you made the choices you did.

Challenge 9B

Task 1

PairWork You are David Glenning, a famous actor. You are being interviewed by a reporter. Use the following information to answer the reporter's questions.

- born in Canada on July 4, 30 years ago
- grew up in Toronto
- as a child: always pretending to be someone else; had tough time—youngest of six boys
- wanted to be a scientist
- can't remember having favorite food
- favorite game—dressing up in grown-ups' clothes
- spent time fighting with older brothers

Task 2

PairWork You are interviewing Sandy Stone, a famous singer, for a magazine article. Find out the following information, and take notes.

- date of birth
- where she grew up
- what she was like as a child
- what she wanted to be
- favorite food
- favorite toy or game
- how she spent her time

you're invited ... *go to the movies!* meet me for lunch
what do you do? why
is my family *neighborhood*

Challenge 12

Task 1

Pair Work Select one of these brochures, but don't tell your partner which one. Imagine you are going to go on vacation to this place. Talk about your plans. Your partner has to guess which place you are going to visit.

Task 2

Pair Work Now change roles and do the task again.

Hong Kong
The City That Never Sleeps
A bustling energy is evident everywhere in Hong Kong. Catch sight of its breathtaking harbor with ships from all over the world. Explore narrow streets where crowds browse at shopping malls beneath imposing skyscrapers. Hong Kong retains an allure that has fascinated the world for centuries.

Fireworks during Chinese New Year add drama to Hong Kong's evening panorama.

Indonesia
Islands of Discovery

The largest archipelago in the world, Indonesia possesses the single most extraordinary collection of wonders on earth. The visitor is faced with limitless opportunities for exploration in Indonesia. Whether your particular interest is hiking through dramatic volcanic landscapes, diving amid colorful coral reefs, seeking out obscure antiquities, or simply relaxing on the beach, Indonesia is out there waiting for you.

Wearing glittering costumes, two young girls perform the traditional Legong Kraton dance.

Challenge 11B

Group Work Work with two other students. You are sharing an apartment with your friends, and you decide to buy a television set. Each of you has a different advertisement. Share your information and decide which set you should buy.

You watch TV late at night, after your friends have gone to bed. You like this set, because it is portable and has a remote control and you can take it to your own room. You don't want to spend more than $500.

$4.35 per week or

$499

Hi-tech portable
remote control color TV
with latest flat screen,
program on/off timer,
full auto search tuning.

Challenge 13A

Pair Work Imagine that you bought one of these items and had some alterations made. The item is delivered in the mail, but it has some things wrong with it. Call the store and talk to the complaints department.

Use structures like the following:

"I want to complain about the suit I bought."
"The .... has/hasn't been ...."
"It has/hasn't been ...."

Woman's designer suit
- hem let down too far
- not clean
- not pressed
- lapel on jacket crushed

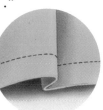
Hem

Lapel

Man's designer suit
- pants taken up too far— legs too short
- not clean
- not pressed
- jacket sleeves too long

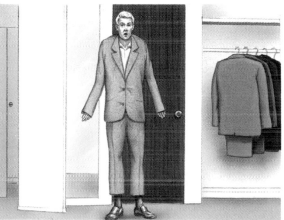

Challenge 14

"Do you like to learn by watching and listening to native speakers?"

Task 1

a PairWork Find out your partner's learning style. If he or she agrees with the statement, check [√] in the box beside it.

How Do You Like to Learn?

Type 1

☐ I like to learn by watching and listening to native speakers.
☐ I like to learn by talking to friends in English.
☐ At home, I like to learn by watching TV and videos in English.
☐ I like to learn by using English outside of class.
☐ I like to learn English words by hearing them.
☐ In class, I like to learn by having conversations.

Total: ………

Type 2

☐ I like the teacher to explain everything to us.
☐ I want to write everything in my notebook.
☐ I like to have my own copy of the textbook.
☐ In class, I like to learn by reading.
☐ I like to study grammar.
☐ I like to learn English words by seeing them.

Total: ………

Type 3

☐ In class, I like to learn by playing games.
☐ In class, I like to learn by looking at pictures, films, and videos.
☐ I like to learn English by talking in pairs.
☐ At home, I like to learn by listening to cassettes.
☐ In class, I like to learn by listening to cassettes.
☐ I like to go out with the class and practice English.

Total: ………

Type 4

☐ I like to study grammar.
☐ At home, I like to learn by studying English books.
☐ I like to study English by myself (alone).
☐ I like the teacher to let me find my mistakes.
☐ I like the teacher to give us problems to work on.
☐ At home, I like to learn by reading newspapers.

Total: ………

b PairWork Now add up the number of check marks for each section, and put the numbers in the *Total* blanks. The highest total shows what kind of learner your partner is.

Task 2

PairWork Now close your book, and answer your partner's questions.

Task 3

GroupWork Compare your responses with another pair's responses.

Task 4

GroupWork Class survey. How many students in the class belong to each category?

Challenge 13B

"Bring the jacket back to the store
and we'll shorten the sleeves."

PairWork Imagine that you work in the complaints department
of a store. You take a telephone call from a customer who is
complaining about some clothing he or she bought and had
altered. Agree to have changes made.

Challenge 11C

GroupWork Work with two other students. You are sharing an
apartment with your friends, and you decide to buy a television set.
Each of you has a different advertisement. Share your information
and decide which set you should buy.

You realize that this TV is expensive, but you like it because you
watch music programs, and you think that the stereo sound would
be an advantage.

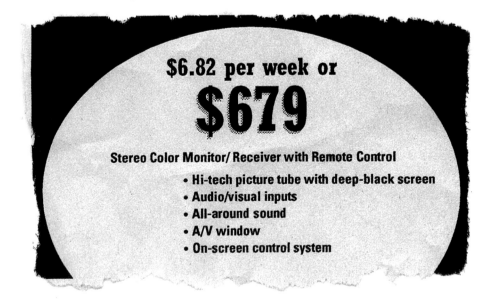

$6.82 per week or

$679

Stereo Color Monitor/ Receiver with Remote Control

- Hi-tech picture tube with deep-black screen
- Audio/visual inputs
- All-around sound
- A/V window
- On-screen control system

Grammar Summaries

Unit 1

1 Relative clauses with *who*

I'm the one who went to school with your husband.
Are you the editor who works with Andre?
He's the guy who asked me to marry him.
She's the woman who called last week.
They're the people who work with Josie.

Jane, who works at the front desk, is a know-it-all.
Scott, who brings around the paychecks, is a nice guy.
Len, who does the mail, is a gossip.
Marcella, who is a word processing operator, knows everybody's good points and bad points.

2 Adjectives ending in *ed* and *ing*

I was disappointed not to get the job.
The job was disappointing.

Everyone was surprised when Tony got fired.
The news about Tony was surprising.

I am exhausted by my job.
My job is exhausting.

Maria is satisfied with the job in Mexico.
The job in Mexico should be satisfying.

Unit 2

1 Past progressive and simple past

Tony and I were arguing when Maria told us to keep quiet.
I was going to bed when Pauline called.
George and I were playing tennis when it started to rain.
I was watching TV when I fell asleep.

2 Requests with *ask* and *tell*

Tell Kim the exam is tomorrow.
Tell the teacher that Tomoko won't be at school today.
Tell Rosa the concert starts at eight.
Tell John to get a new car.

Could you ask Van to pass me the pen?
Ask Sandy to come for dinner tomorrow.
Ask Jim to call me.
Ask Hisako to lend you the book.

Unit 3

1 Modals: *will/won't be able to*

I will be able to see you tomorrow.
He will be able to speak English well at the end of the course.
They won't be able to come to the party on Saturday night.

2 *If* clauses: future events

Probable Events	*Improbable Events*
If it rains, I will get wet.	If it rained, I would get wet.
If she calls, I will let you know.	If she called, I would let you know.
If we hurry, we will catch the bus.	If we hurried, we would catch the bus.

Unit 4

1 Reported speech

Speech	*Reported Speech*
"I'm busy," I said.	I said that I was busy.
"I love movies," said Tom.	Tom said that he loves movies.
"I've been sick," said Nancy.	Nancy said that she had been sick.
"I'll call you later," he said.	He said that he would call me later.
"We have some good friends in L.A."	They said that they had some good friends in L.A.

2 Present perfect progressive

I've been living in Canada for two years.
He's been working as a teacher since graduation.
She's been here all day.
It's been raining all day.
They've been looking for the tomb for months.

Unit 6

1 Requests with *could*, excuses

Could you tell us what you talk about with your best friend?
Could you tell Paul the party starts at eight-thirty?
Could they be here by five?
Could you tell us what you talk about with your friends?

I'm sorry, I can't meet you. I have a dentist's appointment.
I'm sorry, I can't go to the movies with you. I'm going with Paul.

2 *Used to*

I used to eat junk food, but I don't anymore.
He used to listen to the blues, but he doesn't anymore.
She used to watch horror movies, but she doesn't anymore.
We used to go to the Hard Rock Café, but we don't anymore.
They used to read comic books, but they don't anymore.

Unit 7

1 Past perfect

By the time I got to the bus stop, the last bus had left.
When we got to the restaurant, our friends had eaten already.
When Oscar got home last night, he found that someone had broken in.
When Sandy got to the movie, it had already started.
José and Maria were late getting to the airport, and when they got to the boarding gate, the flight had left.

2 Past modal: *should/shouldn't have*

I'm sorry; I should have called you sooner.
He shouldn't have been late for class.
She should have told you she'd be late.
We shouldn't have left the concert early.
They should have left a larger tip.

Unit 8

1 Adjectives and nouns

Someone who is wealthy has wealth.
If someone is aggressive, they have aggression.
If someone is selfish, they have selfishness.
Someone who is angry has anger.
If someone is generous, we say they have generosity.

2 Clauses of reason with *so* and *because*

You have to pay the bride for each dance, so they got a lot of money on their wedding night.
We wanted a cheap wedding because we were poor students when we got married.
A lot of his family wasn't able to come to Miami, so we had another wedding in Mexico City.
We wanted only close friends and family, so we had a small wedding.
My sister got married at Christmas because various members of the family were visiting at the time.

Unit 9

1 Infinitives

Silvia's parents were sorry when she left. They wanted her to stay.
I wanted to leave home. However, my parents persuaded me to stay.
My grandmother doesn't mind growing old. She likes to do things many elderly people do.
Most people don't like to think of old age. They don't like to think about illness or loneliness.
Some young people are very helpful to the elderly. They help to do chores around the home.

2 Superlative adjectives

The most dangerous thing about living where I do is riding the subway late at night.
The most interesting thing about my life is all the different people I get to meet.
The most unusual thing about me is that I speak seven languages.
The most boring aspect of my life is all the studying I have to do.
The least exciting thing about what I do is writing reports for the boss.

Taking the subway is more dangerous than taking the bus.
Being an office worker is less interesting than being a construction worker.
Ita is a more interesting person than Toby, don't you think?
Traveling might be boring, but it's more boring to stay at home.
Writing reports is less exciting than meeting new clients.

ou're invited . . . *to the movies* meet me for lunch
what do you do? why
s my family *neighborhood*

Unit 11

1 Two-part verbs

You weren't in when I called, so I put a message on your answering machine.
The TV's too loud. Could you turn it down, please?
The crossword is difficult. Can you help me fill it in?
The VCR wouldn't work, and then I found I hadn't turned it on.
Frank couldn't work the washing machine, so John wrote out instructions and
    stuck them on the laundry room wall.

2 Indirect questions

Can you tell me where the video store is?
Can you tell him what the advantages are?
Can you tell us what kind of a machine you are looking for?
Can you tell me if it has any disadvantages?
Can you tell me how much it costs?

Unit 12

1 Comparison of adverbs and adjectives

early	earlier	earliest
well	better	best
badly	worse	worst
much	more	most
far	farther	farthest

2 Future: present progressive, *going to*

I'm studying tomorrow.
She's going to meet us at the movies.
He's leaving for South America tomorrow.
We're going to buy a new video player soon.

Unit 13

1 *Would rather, prefer*

I prefer wearing comfortable clothes.
He would rather wear comfortable clothes.
She would rather shop in a department store than in a boutique.
We prefer spending money on entertainment.
They would rather read sports magazines.

2 Passive voice

I was overcharged.
The students were entertained.
She was refunded.
We were kept waiting.
You were insulted.
I was put in the smoking section.
They weren't invited.

Unit 14

1 Prepositional phrases with *by*

I learned Portuguese by living in Brazil.
He learned grammar by memorizing rules.
She memorized vocabulary by taping flash cards to her bedroom mirror.
We improved our pronunciation by working in the language laboratory.
They found out about learning Korean by contacting the local embassy.

2 Word order of modifiers

three old red plastic chairs
a modern silver Japanese vase
two new colorful American paintings
a grey secondhand English sweater
two interesting French poodles

Credits

Photographs

Cover © Allmaps Canada/Rand McNally; © Repolgle Globes; sextant, c. 1810, courtesy Peabody Essex Museum, Salem, MA; photo by Mark Sexton; **9** Tracey Wheeler (cl), (cr), (tl), (cc); PhotoDisc (bl); © Dennis Hallinan/FPG, Int. (bcl); © Richard Hutchings/PhotoEdit (bcr); © Robert E. Daemmrich/Tony Stone Images, Inc. (br); © Jeff Zaruba/AllStock (t); **10** Tracey Wheeler (all); **12** Tracey Wheeler (all); **14** Tracey Wheeler (all); **17** Tracey Wheeler (br), (tl); © Kazuya Shimizu/Photonica (t); **19** Tracey Wheeler (all); **20** Tracey Wheeler (all); **21** Tracey Wheeler (all); **22** Tracey Wheeler (all); **23** Tracey Wheeler (all); **25** PhotoDisc (t); Tracey Wheeler (tl); **29** © Chromosohm/Sohm/Photo Researchers, Inc. (t); © Elizabeth Dawson/Space Biospheres Ventures (b); **30** © Space Biospheres Ventures (t); **31** Tracey Wheeler (all); **33** Permission of AT&T Archives (bl); Collection of Nipper's Choice (tr); George Eastman House (br); Courtesy of American Clock & Watch Museum, Bristol, CT (cr); PhotoDisc (cl); © Masano Kawana/Photonica (t); Tracey Wheeler (tl); **34** Tracey Wheeler (all); **37** Tracey Wheeler (all); **38** Tracey Wheeler (all); **39** Tracey Wheeler (all); **41** Tracey Wheeler (bl), (bc), (br); © Garry Gay/The Image Bank (tl); PhotoDisc (t); **42** Tracey Wheeler (all); **43** Tracey Wheeler (all); **44** Tracey Wheeler (all); **46** Tracey Wheeler (all); **47** Tracey Wheeler (all); **51** © McGee/FPG, Int. (t); Tracey Wheeler (tl); **52** Tracey Wheeler (all); **55** Tracey Wheeler (all); **57** Tracey Wheeler (all); **59** © Robert Brenner/PhotoEdit (bl); © George F. Mobley/National Geographic Society (bc); © Peter Pearson/Tony Stone Images, Inc. (br); Tracey Wheeler (tl); © Ronnie Kaufman/The Stock Market (t); **60** Tracey Wheeler (all); **64** Reuters/Bettmann (t); **65** Tracey Wheeler (all); **67** Tracey Wheeler (cl); **67** Tracey Wheeler (cr), (bl), (bc), (br), (tl); © Dick Luria/FPG, Int. (t); **68** Courtesy Heinle & Heinle (all); **70** © Suzanne Murphy/FPG, Int. (b); **71** © Frederick Lewis/Archive Photos (b); **73** Tracey Wheeler (all); **75** © Garry Gay/The Image Bank (tl); PhotoDisc (t); **77** © Zigy Kaluzny/Tony Stone Images, Inc. (r); © Lightscapes/The Stock Market (t); PhotoDisc (tl); **78** Courtesy of Heinle & Heinle (tl); **78** Courtesy of Heinle & Heinle (t), (tr), (tcl), (tcr), (cl); Tracey Wheeler (cr), (bl), (br); **79** Tracey Wheeler (all); **80** Tracey Wheeler (all); **82** Tracey Wheeler (all); **85** © Deborah Davis/PhotoEdit (cc); © Gerald French/FPG, Int. (cr); © Peter Gridley/FPG, Int. (cl); © Grandadam/Tony Stone Images, Inc. (bcl); PhotoDisc (bc); © Tony Stone Images, Inc. (br), (t); © Bruce Byers/FPG, Int. (bl); © George Hunter/AllStock (tl); **87** © Jeff Zaruba/AllStock (all); **88** © Brian Stablyk/AllStock (t); © John Elk/Tony Stone Images, Inc. (b); **89** © Philip & Karen Smith/ Tony Stone Images, Inc. (t); © Kevin Schafer/AllStock (c); © Vic Bider/PhotoEdit (b); **91** © Telegraph Colour Library/FPG, Int. (t); © Myrleen Ferguson/PhotoEdit (b); **93** Tracey Wheeler (all); **95** © Tony Freeman/PhotoEdit (r); **96** Tracey Wheeler (all); **97** Tracey Wheeler (all); **99** Tracey Wheeler (all); **101** PhotoDisc (cl); PhotoDisc (cc); PhotoDisc (cr); Tracey Wheeler (b), (tl); © Katsumi Suzuki/Photonica (t); **102** Tracey Wheeler (all); **104** Tracey Wheeler (bl); **106** © Gary A. Connor/PhotoEdit (tr); © Tony Freeman/PhotoEdit (cr); **109** Tracey Wheeler (br), (cl), (cr), (cc); © Garry Gay/The Image Bank (tl); PhotoDisc (t); **111** © Tony Stone Images, Inc. (all); **112** © Herman Kokojan/Black Star (all); **123** Tracey Wheeler (all).

Illustrations

All illustrations by Kevin Spaulding.

Text

17 Adapted from Margaret K. Ambry, *1990–1991 Almanac of Consumer Markets.* **25** TV screens adapted from *Fortune,* April 19, 1993; **27** Adapted from *Fortune,* April 19, 1993. Reprinted by permission of *Fortune.* © 1993 Time, Inc. All rights reserved. **45** From *You Just Don't Understand,* by Deborah Tannen, Ph.D. © 1990 by Deborah Tannen, Ph.D. Reprinted by permission of William Morrow & Co., Inc. **47** Adapted from *New Idea,* March 20, 1993. **56** Adapted with permission from *Travel & Leisure,* July 1993. © 1993 American Express Publishing Corporation. All rights reserved. **59** Adapted from L. Dormen, "Will We Last?" *Glamour,* August 1993. Courtesy *Glamour,* © 1993, Condé Nast Publications, Inc. **69** Adapted from *Parade Magazine,* December 12, 1993, p. 4. Adapted with permission of Mark Clements Research, Inc. and Parade Publications. © 1993. All rights reserved. **87** Adapted from *The Official Hong Kong Guide,* published by the Hong Kong Tourist Association. Adapted with permission of the Hong Kong Tourist Association. © 1993. **95** Adapted from *Glamour,* August 1993, p. 180. Courtesy *Glamour,* © 1993, Condé Nast Publications, Inc. **126** Adapted from Ken Willing, *Teaching How to Learn,* by permission of the National Centre for English Language Training and Research, Sydney.

Irregular Verb Chart

SIMPLE FORM ►	PAST FORM ►	PAST PARTICIPLE
arise	arose	arisen
be	was	been
begin	began	begun
bite	bit	bitten
blow	blew	blown
break	broke	broken
bring	brought	brought
build	built	built
buy	bought	bought
catch	caught	caught
choose	chose	chosen
cost	cost	cost
cut	cut	cut
do	did	done
draw	drew	drawn
drink	drank	drunk
drive	drove	driven
eat	ate	eaten
fall	fell	fallen
feed	fed	fed
feel	felt	felt
fight	fought	fought
find	found	found
fly	flew	flown
forget	forgot	forgotten
get	got	gotten
give	gave	given
go	went	gone
grow	grew	grown
have	had	had
hear	heard	heard
hold	held	held
keep	kept	kept
know	knew	known
learn	learned	learned
leave	left	left

SIMPLE FORM ►	PAST FORM ►	PAST PARTICIPLE
let	let	let
light	lit	lit
lose	lost	lost
make	made	made
mean	meant	meant
meet	met	met
pay	paid	paid
put	put	put
read	read	read
ride	rode	ridden
ring	rang	rung
run	ran	run
say	said	said
see	saw	seen
sell	sold	sold
send	sent	sent
shoot	shot	shot
show	showed	shown
shut	shut	shut
sing	sang	sung
sink	sank	sunk
sit	sat	sat
sleep	slept	slept
speak	spoke	spoken
stand	stood	stood
swim	swam	swum
take	took	taken
teach	taught	taught
tell	told	told
think	thought	thought
throw	threw	thrown
understand	understood	understood
wake	woke	woken
wear	wore	worn
win	won	won
write	wrote	written